P9-ELS-653

HANDBOOK

FOR

TODAY'S
CATHOLIC

Fully indexed to the
Catechism of the Catholic Church

Revised Edition

A REDEMPTORIST
PASTORAL PUBLICATION

FOREWORD BY
FRANCIS CARDINAL GEORGE

Liguori
ONE LIGUORI DRIVE
LIGUORI MO 63057-9999

Imprimi Potest:
Richard Thibodeau, C.Ss.R.
Provincial, Denver Province
The Redemptorists

Imprimatur:
Most Reverend Robert J. Hermann
Auxiliary Bishop
Archdiocese of St. Louis

ISBN 978-0-7648-1220-0
Library of Congress Catalog Card Number: 2004107426

Scripture selections taken from the *New American Bible With Revised New Testament*, copyright © 1986, by the Confraternity of Christian Doctrine, 3211 Fourth Street, Washington, DC 20017-1194, and are used with permission. All rights reserved.

Excerpts from *Vatican II: The Basic Sixteen Documents Vatican Council II,* edited by Austin Flannery, O.P., copyright © 1996, Austin P. Flannery, O.P. are used by permission of the publisher. All rights reserved.

Excerpts from the English translation of the *Catechism of the Catholic Church* for the United States of America, © 1994, United States Catholic Conference, Inc.—Libreria Editrice Vaticana. Used with permission.

Excerpts from the English translation of the *Rite of Penance,* copyright © 1974, International Committee on English in the Liturgy (ICEL), are used with permission. All rights reserved.

Liguori Publications, a nonprofit corporation, is an apostolate of the Redemptorists. To learn more about the Redemptorists, visit Redemptorists.com.

To order, call 1-800-325-9521
www.liguori.org

CONTENTS

Foreword • 9
Introduction • 11

SECTION ONE: BELIEFS

1. **You the Seeker, God the Seeker • 15**
   You: A Human Being Who Seeks God • 15
   God: The Divine Lover Who Found You • 16

2. **Revelation, Faith, Doctrine, and Doubt • 17**
   Revelation and Faith • 17
   Catholic Doctrine • 17
   Faith and Doubt • 18

3. **One God, Three Divine Persons • 19**
   Three Persons, One God • 19
   Creator, Savior, Sanctifier • 20

4. **God, the Father of Jesus • 21**

5. **Jesus Christ • 23**
   Jesus, God and Man • 23
   Christ, the Revelation and Sacrament of God • 25
   Christ, the Center of Your Life • 25

6. **The Holy Spirit • 26**
    The Indwelling Spirit • 26
    Gifts of the Spirit • 27
7. **Grace and the Theological Virtues • 28**
    Grace: God's Life Within You • 28
    Faith, Hope, and Charity • 29
    Love for God, Self, Others • 30
8. **The Catholic Church • 31**
    The Church: Founded by Jesus Christ • 31
    The Church as the Body of Christ • 34
    The Church as the Sacrament of Christ • 34
    The Catholic People of God • 35
    The Catholic Church: A Unique Institution • 36
    Infallibility in the Church • 38
9. **Mary, Mother of Jesus and of the Church • 39**
10. **The Saints • 41**
11. **The Scriptures and Tradition • 41**
    The Bible: Its Books and Its Message • 42
    Tradition, Vatican II, and Parents • 44
12. **Sin: Original and Personal • 46**
    The Original Sin and Its Effects • 46
    Personal Sin • 48
    Personal Sin and Social Evil • 49
    Formation of a Correct Conscience • 50
13. **The Sacraments of the Church • 51**
    Baptism: New Life and Ways of Living • 51
    Confirmation: Seal of the Spirit, Gift of the Father • 53
    Eucharist: Sacrifice and Sacrament • 54
    Penance: Reconciliation • 56
    Anointing of the Sick • 57

Holy Orders: Ministerial Priesthood • 58
Matrimony: Sacrament of Life-giving Oneness • 60

14. Human Destiny • 62
Individual Death and Judgment • 62
Purgatory and the Communion of Saints • 63
Hell • 64
Heaven • 65
A New Earth and a New Heaven • 66

SECTION TWO: PRACTICES

1. **God's Two Great Commandments • 69**
2. **Commandments of God • 69**
3. **Precepts of the Church • 71**
4. **Holy Days of Obligation • 72**
5. **Regulations for Fast and Abstinence • 74**
6. **Confession of Sins • 75**
7. **Regulations for the Communion Fast • 77**
8. **How to Receive Communion • 77**
9. **Beatitudes • 78**
10. **Corporal (Material) Works of Mercy • 80**
11. **Spiritual Works of Mercy • 80**
12. **How to Baptize in Case of an Emergency • 81**
13. **How to Prepare for a Sick Call (Reconciliation, Communion, Anointing) • 81**
14. **Liturgical Seasons of the Year • 82**

SECTION THREE: PRAYERS

Introductory Note • 85

1. **Sign of the Cross • 86**
2. **Our Father • 86**
3. **Hail Mary • 86**
4. **Prayer of Praise (Doxology) • 87**
5. **Grace Before and Thanksgiving After Meals • 87**
6. **Morning Offering • 87**
7. **Act of Faith • 88**
8. **Act of Hope • 88**
9. **Act of Love • 89**
10. **Act of Contrition • 89**
11. **Come, Holy Spirit • 90**
12. **Prayer for Vocations • 90**
13. **Prayer to Your Guardian Angel • 90**
14. **Prayer for the Faithful Departed • 91**
15. **Stations of the Cross • 91**
16. **Prayer to Jesus Christ Crucified • 92**
17. **Prayer to Our Redeemer • 92**
18. **Memorare • 93**
19. **Angelus • 93**
20. **Queen of Heaven • 94**
21. **Hail, Holy Queen • 95**
22. **Mary's Rosary • 96**
23. **The Nicene Creed • 99**
24. **Apostles' Creed • 100**

25. **Benediction of the Most Blessed Sacrament
     (Prayer to Christ in the Eucharist) • 100**

26. **Order of the Mass (Community Prayer) • 103**

27. **A Method of Meditation (Private Prayer) • 104
     Further Suggestions for Meditative Prayer • 106**

SECTION FOUR: LIVING THE FAITH IN THE SPIRIT OF VATICAN II

Sacred Scripture • 108
> Scripture in the Life of the Church and the Believer • 108
> The Interpretation of Scripture and Fundamentalism • 109
> The Bible Is a Prayer Book • 110

Liturgy and Worship • 111
> Celebration of Mass • 111
> The Sacraments • 113

Called to Ministry • 116
> Social Justice • 117
> Adult Faith Formation • 118
> Evangelization • 121
> Spread the Good News • 122
> To Announce the Good News—the RCIA • 123
> Unity Among Believers • 124

In the Spirit of the Council • 125

FOREWORD

The intention of this booklet is to help us grow in faith and love. To be a Christian is to embrace and live the truth revealed by God in Jesus Christ. This truth is handed on securely in the Tradition and the Scriptures of the Catholic Church by means of the teaching office with which Christ endowed his Church. Pope John Paul II's call for a new evangelization is prompted by the silent loss of faith in a large part of Christianity. Faith is replaced often by a tolerance which makes all truth relative.

No one is Catholic on his or her own terms: not the pope, not bishops or priests, not religious, not laypeople. It is necessary to accept with integrity the body of belief which the Church, the Body of Christ, holds to be true. Whether one is a member of the company of believers or a theologian or teacher of the apostolic faith in it, all of us are bound by the Church's rule of faith. It is not enough for an individual to read the Bible, praiseworthy though that is in itself, in order to grasp the meaning of what is in those inspired texts. It is necessary to do so in light of the faith of the Church. There are aspects of understanding which become available to the individual only because the Church's Tradition makes them intelligible.

This booklet carries in it a selection of Catholic prayers. We cannot know Christ, we cannot live the faith of the Church without prayer, which unites our hearts to God. It is essential to accept the truths of the faith, but those truths have to become one's own personal adhesion to God in Christ by the power of the Holy Spirit. The objective truth of the faith has to be interiorized to become the basis of a personal relationship with Jesus Christ that will change and shape one's life. Here and now one must begin to live by the knowledge that one day will be the vision of God in heaven.

This little book comes as a challenge to Catholics to be alert to contemporary difficulties of belief. It is a support in living the faith. It is an invitation to keep close to the teaching of the Church in order to draw closer to God. The immediate source of the teaching set out here is the *Catechism of the Catholic Church*, which is the "new authoritative exposition of the one and perennial apostolic faith." The *Catechism* is "a sure norm for teaching the faith" and remains the basic text; a useful piece of writing such as the present booklet simply helps make some of its teaching more accessible not claiming to be complete or to cover all important questions equally well. It can, however, serve to lead the reader to the text of the *Catechism.* May the reader use it well and grow in faith and love.

Francis Cardinal George, O.M.I.
Archbishop of Chicago

INTRODUCTION

We live in a new century. We live in a place where we can explore the planets around us and talk about living on the moon. This is much different from the beginning of the twentieth century. That was a century of dreams and plans and promise. Sometimes the dreams succeeded beyond all expectation. For most of the twentieth century the Catholic Church stood as a seemingly unchanging reality that helped us keep our balance.

The Catholic Church in the third millennium is both different from the Church of the twentieth century and the same as that Church. The Second Vatican Council in the second half of the twentieth century set the Church on a path of renewal. In the midst of that renewal, we look to the unchanging things that we believe and the developing ways in which we can express those beliefs.

The purpose of this handbook is to look at some basic doctrines of the Catholic Church and explain them for the present generation. Here you will find the unchanging truths revealed by God seen through the filter of modern culture. There is no new teaching here. There is no ambiguous explanation. There is today's language and scholarship explaining the truths from Genesis to Revelation. The explanations are faithful to the great ecumenical council of our age, Vatican II.

You will also find in these pages some of the prayers and practices of the Catholic Church. These things do change, of course, over the centuries. Each culture and age finds appropriate ways of celebrating Mass, praying to God, and honoring the saints. The essentials, though, do not change.

One of the great projects of the Church in the past century was to prepare and publish a universal *Catechism of the Catholic Church*. This edition of the *Handbook* is fully indexed to the *Catechism*. The numbers found in square brackets, "[ ]," refer you to specific articles in the Catechism. You will also find references to documents from Vatican II cited in the text where appropriate.

Section One: Beliefs. This section relies upon the Nicene Creed, the summary of our beliefs as Catholics, to explain the revelation Jesus gives us. In this part of the *Handbook* are the teachings about Jesus, the Holy Trinity, the Church, the sacraments, and other basic dogmas that Catholics believe and by which they live.

Section Two: Practices. Here you will find the fundamental moral teaching of the Church. Morality is about how we behave—how we act—in this world. The basis of the moral teaching is the Ten Commandments, but the precepts of the Church are also mentioned here. There are some practical points about sacraments, holy days, and some other elements of Catholic practices.

Section Three: Prayers. Prayer is communication with God. As individuals we pray and as the universal Church we pray together in our liturgy. Section Three offers some prayers common to Catholics.

Section Four: Living the Faith in the Spirit of Vatican II. This expanded section of the *Handbook* explains the influence Vatican II continues to have on Catholic practice and belief. The Church after Vatican II is one that offers expanded roles for the laity in the Church. This council also emphasized the importance of the liturgy in the life of the Church and called for renewal of our understanding of Scripture, sacraments, social responsibility, faith formation, and evangelization. This section also treats the Rite of Christian Initiation of Adults that was renewed and expanded after the Council.

BELIEFS

1. You the Seeker, God the Seeker

Man is by nature and vocation a religious being. Coming from God, going toward God, man lives a fully human life only if he freely lives by his bond with God.

CATECHISM OF THE CATHOLIC CHURCH, 44

You: A Human Being
Who Seeks God

[1, 1701-1715]

As a human person you ask questions and you make decisions. You wonder about things, which is where your questions come from, and you choose what to do and how to act, which are your decisions. These two things reveal that you have a *free will* that enables you to choose, and a questioning *intellect* [1-3].

> *The ultimate reality you seek...is God.*

Things change over time. The way you look, the way you view life will change. At your core, you do not change. You are constantly reaching out, seeking that for which you were created. This questing, spiritual core of your being has been called by many names. Common names for it are *soul*, *spirit*, or *heart* [27, 44-47].

The Ultimate Reality you seek—which is present in ·everything you reach out to—has also been called by many names. The most common name for this Ultimate Reality is *God* [43]. You are so bound to God that without him you would not live or move or have your being. You are so bound to God that if you did not sense his presence in some way, you would view life as pointless and cease to seek... [1701-1715, 1718].

God: The Divine Lover
Who Found You
[50-53, 142, 1719]

Meanwhile, as you seek God, God seeks you. The Vatican II *Dogmatic Constitution on Divine Revelation* expresses it this way: "The invisible God, from the fullness of his love, addresses men and women as his friends, and lives among them, in order to invite and receive them into his own company" (2) [1719].

As a Catholic you are called to seek and find Christ. But you did not begin this quest on your own initiative. The initiative was all God's. All who follow Christ were once lost but were searched for and found. God first found you and made you visibly his in baptism. What he seeks now is that you seek him. In a mysterious way your whole life with God is an

ongoing quest for each other by two lovers—God and you—
who already possess each other [50-53, 521].

2. Revelation, Faith, Doctrine, and Doubt

*God wished to manifest and communicate both him-
self and the eternal decrees of his will concerning
the salvation of humankind.*

DOGMATIC CONSTITUTION ON DIVINE REVELATION, 6

Revelation and Faith

[50-64]

In revealing, God has not only communicated information; he has communicated *himself* to you. Your personal
response to God's communication of himself and his will is
called *faith*. "By faith one freely commits oneself entirely to
God, making 'the full submission of intellect and will to God
who reveals,' and willingly assenting to the revelation given
by God" (*Dogmatic Constitution on Divine Revelation*, 5)
[36-38, 51-53, 142, 143, 153-164, 1814-1816].

Catholic Doctrine

[84-100]

The words we use to explain what God has revealed to us
about our relationship with him are called doctrines or
dogmas. The key characteristic of the Church's dogmas is
that they agree with sacred Scripture. The teachings communicate the unchangeable content of revelation by using the
changeable thought-forms and languages of people in every

new era and culture. A dogma is a statement of truth, a formulation of some aspect of the faith. As a coherent set of teachings, Church dogma is a faithful interpretation of God's self-communication to humankind [88-100, 170-171].

Faith and Doubt

The Church's dogmatic formulas, however, are not the same thing as God's self-revelation; they are the way in which Catholics express their faith in God and pass it on. God unveils and communicates the hidden mystery of himself *through* Church teachings. The teachings are like sacraments through which you receive God. Through the medium of doctrinal formulas, you reach God himself in the personal act of faith [88-90, 170].

> *The key characteristic of the Church's dogmas is that they agree with Sacred Scripture.*

The life of faith is very personal and delicate—and ultimately mysterious. Faith is a gift of God. A person can lack faith through his or her own fault; we are free—even to reject God. But when a person "doubts," we should not jump to conclusions. For example, some people cannot bring themselves to believe in God as their "good Father" because of painful memories of their own father. This is not a lack of faith. They have no context that lets them appreciate God as Father. Negative memories can block a person from receiving God's self-revelation in a particular form. But such images cannot block out all forms in which people perceive and express God's mystery. God seeks us until we find him [153, 215].

A person seeking deeper insight may sometimes have doubts, even about God himself. Such doubts do not necessarily indicate a lack of faith. In fact, they may be a sign of growing faith. Faith is alive and dynamic. It seeks, through grace, to penetrate into the very mystery of God. Faith is a living gift that must be nourished by the word of God. Even when inclined to reject a particular doctrine, the person should go right on seeking the revealed truth expressed by the doctrine. When in doubt, "Seek and you will find." The person who seeks by reading, discussing, thinking, or praying eventually sees light. The person who talks to God even when God is "not there" is alive with faith [162].

3. One God, Three Divine Persons

[232-267]

The Father is God, the Son is God, and the Holy Spirit is God, and yet there are not three gods but one God.

ATHANASIAN CREED

The Catholic Church teaches that the fathomless mystery we call God has revealed himself to humankind as a Trinity of Persons—the Father, the Son, and the Holy Spirit [238-248].

Three Persons, One God

[249-267]

The mystery of the Trinity is the central doctrine of Catholic faith. Upon it are based all other teachings of the Church. In the New Testament there is frequent mention of the Father, the Son, and the Holy Spirit. A careful reading of these passages leads to one unmistakable conclusion: each Person is

19

presented as having qualities that can belong only to God. But if there is only one God, how can this be [199-202]?

> *The mystery of the Trinity is the central doctrine of Catholic faith.*

The Church studied this mystery with great care and, after four centuries of clarification, decided to state the doctrine in this way: in the unity of the Godhead there are three Persons—the Father, the Son, and the Holy Spirit—truly distinct one from another [249-256].

Creator, Savior, Sanctifier
[257-260]

All effects of God's action upon his creatures are produced by the three divine Persons in common. But because certain effects of the divine action in creation remind us more of one divine Person than another, the Church ascribes particular effects to one or the other divine Person. Thus, we speak of the Father as Creator of all that is, of the Son, the Word of God, as our Savior or Redeemer, and of the Holy Spirit—the love of God "poured into our hearts"—as our Sanctifier [234-237].

To believe that God is Father means to believe that you are son or daughter; that God your Father accepts and loves you; that God your Father has created you as a love-worthy human being [238-240].

To believe that God is saving Word means to believe that you are a listener; that your response to God's Word is to open yourself to his liberating gospel which frees you to choose union with God and brotherhood with your neighbor [2716, 2724].

To believe that God is Spirit means to believe that on this earth you are meant to live a sanctifying, supernatural life that is a created sharing in God's own nature—a life which is the beginning of life eternal [1691, 1703, 1704].

4. God, the Father of Jesus
[198-267]

The Incarnation of God's Son reveals that God is the eternal Father...the Son is one and the same God.

CATECHISM OF THE CATHOLIC CHURCH, 262

The Book of Exodus records one of the most profound revelations in human history. The revelation is narrated in the story of God calling Moses to be the leader of his people. Speaking from a burning bush, which "though on fire, was not consumed," God called out: "Moses! Moses!" God then told Moses to organize the Israelites and persuade Pharaoh to let him lead that enslaved people out of Egypt. Hearing the plan, Moses was apprehensive. The dialogue goes [204, 210, 211]:

"But," said Moses to God, "when I go to the Israelites and say to them, 'The God of your fathers has sent me to you,' if they ask me, 'What is his name?' what am I to tell them?" God replied, "I am who am." Then he added, "This is what you shall tell the Israelites: I AM sent me to you" [446, 2575].

God spoke further to Moses, "Thus shall you say to the Israelites: The LORD, the God of your fathers, the God of Abraham, the God of Isaac, the God of Jacob, has sent me to you."

EXODUS 3:13-15

In this dialogue God does not really give himself a "name." God says, in effect, that he is not like any of the many gods people worship. He conceals himself—thereby revealing the infinite distance between himself and all that we human beings try to know and control [205-209].

But by telling Moses to say, "I AM sent me to you," God also reveals something very personal. This God who "is," beyond all realities that come and go, is connected with us and our world. This God who "is" reveals that he is *with you*. He does not tell *what* he is *in himself*. But he does reveal *who* he is *to you*. In this key moment recorded in Exodus (and developed further in the Book of Isaiah, chapters 40-45), God revealed that he is *your* God, the "God of your fathers"—the fathomless mystery who is with you through all time, with you beyond all powers of death and evil [214-221, 2810].

The God who reveals himself in the Old Testament has two main characteristics. First, and most important, is the revelation that he is personally close to you, that he is *your* God. Second, this God who freely chooses a personal relationship with you is beyond all time and space. I AM is bound to nothing, but binds all things to himself. In his own words, "I am the first and I am the last; / there is no God but me" (Isaiah 44:6) [198, 212].

Centuries after the revelation reflected in Exodus and Isaiah, the mysterious God of the burning bush did reveal his name—in Person. Shattering all human assumptions and expectations, God's Word "became flesh and made his dwelling among us" (John 1:14) [65, 73]. In a revelation that blinds the mind with its light, Jesus spoke to I AM and said: "Father, [you] are in me and I in you...I made known to them your name and I will make it known, that the love with which you loved me may be in them and I in them" (John 17:21,26) [260, 422-425, 820, 2750].

I AM reveals his name in his Son. The burning bush draws you into its light. The God of Moses, revealed in Jesus, is love, is Father, is in you [211, 218-221, 587-591].

5. Jesus Christ

[422-682]

We believe and confess that Jesus of Nazareth...is the eternal Son of God made man.

CATECHISM OF THE CATHOLIC CHURCH, 423

Jesus, God and Man

[464-469]

The second Person of the Blessed Trinity became a man, Jesus Christ. His mother was Mary of Nazareth. Joseph, Mary's husband, was like a father to Jesus but Jesus' true and only Father is God; he had no human father [525, 526].

Conceived in Mary's womb by the power of the Holy Spirit, Jesus was born in Bethlehem of Judea, probably between the years 6 and 4 B.C. [484, 487]. He died on Calvary (outside of Old Jerusalem) as a relatively young man, most likely in his early thirties [595-623].

He is only one Person, but he has both a divine nature and a human nature. He is truly God, and he is also truly a human being. As God, he has all the qualities and attributes of God. As human, he has a human body, human soul, human mind and will, human imagination, and human feelings. His divinity does not overwhelm or interfere with his humanity—and vice versa [464-478].

On Calvary he really died; he experienced the same kind of death that all human beings experience. But during his dying, at his death, and after his death, he remained God [595-623].

After his death, Jesus "descended to the dead." The older English translation of the Creed said "descended into hell"— which means the same thing: *Hades*, the nether world, the region of the dead, the condition of those who had passed on from this life. (This is clear from New Testament references such as 1 Peter 3:19ff, 4:6; Ephesians 4:9; Romans 10:7; Matthew 12:40; Acts 2:27,31.) Basically, therefore, "descended to the dead" means Jesus really died and entered among the dead as their Savior. Liturgically, Holy Saturday expresses this aspect of the mystery of salvation—the "death" or absence of God [631-637].

The prayer of the dying Jesus—"My God, my God, why have you forsaken me?" (Mark 15:34)—finds its echo in the lives of many Christians. "Descended to the dead" expresses Jesus' outcry of agony—his experience of clinging to his Father in his moment of absolute anguish. It also expresses what many Catholics experience as God deepens their love of him by making them realize the hell life is without a sense of his presence [618].

Jesus rose from the dead on Easter morning. He is living

today with his Father and the Spirit—and in our midst. He is still both God and man and always will be [638-658].

He lives. And his passage from death to life is the mystery of salvation we are all meant to share [655, 658].

Christ, the Revelation and Sacrament of God

[65-67]

By his preaching, and by his death and resurrection, Jesus is both the revealer and the *revelation of God*. Who the Father is, is shown in his Son, Jesus. As the revelation of God, Jesus is both God's approach to humankind and our path to God [73, 422-425].

Jesus is the ultimate sign of God's salvation in the world— the center and means of God's encounter with you. We call him the *original sacrament.* The grace he communicates to you is himself. Through this communication of himself, you receive the total self-communication of God. Jesus is the saving presence of God in the world [519, 520, 1113-1116].

> *Jesus is the ultimate sign... of God's encounter with you.*

Christ, the Center of Your Life

[426-429]

Jesus comes to you, actively influencing your life in various ways. He comes to you in his Word—when the Word of God is preached to you or when you read the Scriptures with attentive reverence [101-104]. He is present to you in the seven sacraments—especially in the Eucharist [1373].

Another way you meet Jesus is in other people. As we read in the final judgment scene in the gospel, "Then the righteous will answer him and say, 'Lord, when did we see you hungry and feed you, or thirsty and give you drink?'...And the king will say to them in reply, 'Amen, I say to you, whatever you did for one of these least brothers of mine, you did for me'" (Matthew 25:37,40) [678, 1503, 1939, 2449].

The Catholic Church believes that Jesus of Nazareth is the center of our lives and destiny. Vatican II affirms that Jesus is "the key, the center and the purpose of the whole of human history" (*Pastoral Constitution on the Church in the Modern World,* 10). With Saint Paul, the Church believes that "many are the promises of God, their Yes is in him" (2 Corinthians 1:20) [65-73, 426-429].

6. The Holy Spirit

[683-747]

The One whom the Father has sent into our hearts, the Spirit of his Son, is truly God.

CATECHISM OF THE CATHOLIC CHURCH, 689

The Indwelling Spirit

There is a common way in which God is present to all of creation. Saint Paul referred to this all-enveloping presence of God when he quoted a Greek poet who said, "In him we live and move and have our being" (Acts 17:28) [28, 300].

But there is another entirely personal presence of God within those who love him. Jesus says: "Whoever loves me will keep my word, and my Father will love him, and we will come to him and make our dwelling with him" (John 14:23) [260].

This special presence of the Trinity is the work of the Holy Spirit, for as Saint Paul proclaims, "The love of God has been poured out into our hearts through the holy Spirit that has been given to us" (Romans 5:5). This presence of the Spirit, God's gift of love within you, is called the *divine indwelling* [733].

Gifts of the Spirit
[1830-1832]

The Spirit is not only intimately present within you; he is silently but actively working to transform you. If you pay attention to his silent promptings, then you will experience the gifts of the Holy Spirit.

The seven gifts of the Holy Spirit are permanent supernatural qualities that enable the graced person to be especially in tune with the inspirations of the Holy Spirit. These gifts make us holy. They are **wisdom** (which helps a person value the things of heaven), **understanding** (which enables the person to grasp the truths of religion), **counsel** (which helps one see and correctly choose the best practical approach in serving God), **fortitude** (which steels a person's resolve in overcoming obstacles to living the faith), **knowledge** (which helps one see the path to follow and the dangers to one's faith), **piety** (which fills a person with confidence in God and an eagerness to serve him), and **fear of the Lord** (which makes a person keenly aware of God's sovereignty and the respect due to him and his laws) [1830, 1831, 1845].

A second kind of gifts of the Spirit are called charisms. They are extraordinary favors granted principally for the help

27

of others. In 1 Corinthians 12:6-11, nine charisms are mentioned. They are the gifts of **speaking with wisdom, speaking with knowledge, faith, healing, miracles, prophecy, discerning of spirits, tongues,** and **interpreting speeches** [688, 799-801, 809].

Other passages of Saint Paul (such as 1 Corinthians 12:28-31 and Romans 12:6-8) mention other charisms [736, 1508, 2004].

7. Grace and the Theological Virtues
[1996-2005, 1812-1829]

Grace is the help God gives us to respond to our vocation....

CATECHISM OF THE CATHOLIC CHURCH, 2021

Grace: God's Life Within You
[1996-2005]

Grace is the Spirit of God who is "poured out into our hearts" (Romans 5:5). The Church makes a distinction between habitual or sanctifying grace and actual grace which helps us do the right thing [368, 733].

Grace, the presence to you of God's living, dynamic Spirit, helps you to live with a new, abundant inner life that makes you "share in the divine nature" (2 Peter 1:4), as a son or daughter of God, and a brother or sister—a fellow heir—with Jesus, "the firstborn among many brothers" [357]. (See Romans, chapter 8.)

The Spirit's presence helps you live and respond to God in a totally new way. You live a "graced" life that is good, really pleasing to God. Under the Spirit's influence you live a life of love that builds up Christ's Body, the Church. Being "in the Spirit" with the rest of the Church, you live with others in such a way as to build a spirit of love and community wherever you are [1721, 1810].

Grace—God's life within you—transforms the whole meaning and direction of your life [1722, 1810]. In grace, Saint Paul declared: "For to me life is Christ, and death is gain" (Philippians 1:21) [1010, 1698]. Ultimately, grace—God's free gift of himself to you—is life eternal, a life that has already begun. Already, while you are still an earthly pilgrim, grace is "Christ in you, the hope for glory" (Colossians 1:27) [772].

> *Grace...*
> *transforms the*
> *whole meaning*
> *and direction*
> *of your life.*

Faith, Hope, and Charity
[1812-1829]

As a human being, you are capable of believing, trusting, and loving others. Grace transforms these ways you relate to others into the theological (God-directed) virtues of faith, hope, and charity—capacities to relate to God and others as one of his dearly loved sons and daughters [1810].

In the state of grace, you have *faith*: you believe in God, committing your total being to him as the personal source of all truth and reality and your own being. You have *hope*: you rest your whole meaning and future on God, whose promise to you of life everlasting with him is being fulfilled in a hidden manner even now through your graced existence. And you have *charity*: you love God as the personal *All* of your life and all persons as sharers in the destiny God desires for all—everlasting communion with himself [2086-2094].

If people alienate themselves from God by serious sin, they lose habitual grace and the virtue of charity. But this loss does not take away their faith or hope unless they sin directly and seriously against these virtues.

Love for God, Self, Others
[2083]

In this life, your love for God is bound together with your love of others—and these loves are bound together with your love of self. "Whoever does not love a brother whom he has seen cannot love God whom he has not seen" (1 John 4:20) [2840]. And by God's own commandment, you are to love your neighbor *as yourself* (Matthew 19:19; 22:39) [2052]. When it comes to practical, real-life terms, fulfillment of God's commandment to love begins with a proper self-love. In order to love God as he wills, you need to respect, esteem, and reverence yourself [2055].

You increase your love of self by allowing yourself to realize, gradually and more deeply as the years go on, that *God really loves you* with a love that has no end. You are loved and you are lovable. Whenever you try to acquire or deepen this attitude about yourself, you are cooperating with the grace of God [2196].

You also increase your love for self by better understanding those around you. You listen to others, trust them, and love them. You let yourself *be* loved, by being truly forgiving and (what is most difficult) seeking true personal forgiveness, by widening your circle of compassion to embrace all living creatures and the whole of nature in its beauty [2842-2845].

Saint John writes about the importance of love: "Beloved, let us love one another, because love is of God; everyone who loves is begotten by God and knows God. Whoever is without love does not know God, for God is love" (1 John 4:7-8). You learn what love is by loving. By loving, you come to know God [1, 214, 221, 773, 1828].

8. The Catholic Church

[748-870]

The Father...determined to call together in the holy church those who believe in Christ.

DOGMATIC CONSTITUTION ON THE CHURCH, 2

The Church: Founded by Jesus Christ

[763-766]

The whole life of Jesus, the Word made flesh, was the foundation of the Church [514-521]. Jesus gathered to himself followers who committed themselves completely to him. Praying beforehand, Jesus then chose his inner circle—the Twelve. To the Twelve he disclosed personal knowledge of himself, spoke of his coming passion and death, and gave in-depth instruction regarding what following his way entailed. Only the Twelve were allowed to celebrate his Last Supper with him [1340].

The Twelve were called *apostles*—that is, emissaries whose mission was to be Jesus' personal representatives.

He gave these apostles the full power of authority he had from the Father: "Amen, I say to you, whatever you bind on earth shall be bound in heaven, and whatever you loose on earth shall be loosed in heaven" (Matthew 18:18) [2, 75-77, 126].

The climax of Jesus' preparation for the Church was the Last Supper. At this meal he took bread and wine and said: "Take and eat, this is my body: take and drink, this is my blood." With these words he actually gave *himself* to them. Receiving him in this way, the Twelve entered into a union of such total intimacy with him and with one another that nothing like it had ever before taken place. At that meal they became *one body in Jesus.* Saint Paul expresses this profound communion that the Church has with Jesus: "Because the loaf of bread is one, we, though many, are one body, for we all partake of the one loaf" (1 Corinthians 10:17) [610, 1396].

At the Supper, Jesus also spoke of the "new testament." God was establishing a new relationship with humankind, a covenant sealed with the sacrificial blood of Christ himself. This new relationship was to be governed by a new law—the commandment of love [1339].

The earliest account of the Eucharist, in First Corinthians, reveals what the Last Supper meant for the future of the Church. Jesus is recorded as saying, "Do this in remembrance of me" (11:24). Jesus foresaw a long time in which his presence would not be visible to his followers. He intended that the Church repeat this Supper again and again during that time. In these memorials he would be intimately present, the risen Lord of history leading his people toward that future day when he will "make all things new" (Revelation 21:5) [1044, 1323, 1341-1344].

The Last Supper was Jesus' final step before his death in preparing the Twelve. This celebration revealed how they, and their successors through the ages, were to carry out his mission of teaching, sanctifying, and governing.

According to the gospels (Matthew 16:13-19; Luke 22:31ff; John 21:15-17), the responsibility given to the apostles was given in a special way to Saint Peter. Jesus's words are: "And so I say to you, you are Peter, and upon this rock I will build my church, and the gates of the netherworld shall not prevail against it" (Matthew 16:18). Peter is to be the visible representative of Jesus, who is the foundation of the Church. Peter is to provide the Church with unshakable leadership against any forces that would destroy what Jesus brings to his people [552, 553, 567].

Jesus' founding of the Church was completed with the sending of the Holy Spirit. The actual birth of the Church took place on the day of Pentecost. This sending of the Spirit took place publicly, just as the crucifixion of Jesus took place in public view. Since that day, the Church has shown itself to be a divine-human reality—a combination of the Spirit working and the people striving, in their human way, to co-operate with the gift of his presence and Christ's gospel [731, 732, 767, 768].

The climax of Jesus' preparation for the Church was the Last Supper.

The Church as the Body of Christ

[787-796]

The image of the Church as the Body of Christ is found in the New Testament writings of Saint Paul. In chapter 10 of 1 Corinthians, Paul says that our communion with Christ comes from "the cup of blessing," which unites us in his blood, and from "the bread that we break," which unites us to his body. Because the bread is one, all of us, though many, are one body. The eucharistic body of Christ and the Church are, together, the (Mystical) Body of Christ [805-807].

In chapter 12 of both 1 Corinthians and Romans, Paul emphasizes the mutual dependence and concern we have as *members of one another*. In the Letters to the Ephesians and Colossians, the emphasis is on *Christ as our head.* God gave Christ to the Church as its head. Through Christ, God is unfolding his plan, "the mystery hidden for ages," to unite all things and to reconcile us to himself. Because this mystery is being unfolded in the Church, Ephesians calls the Church the *mystery of Christ* [669, 770-776].

The Church as the Sacrament of Christ

[774-776, 780]

In our own time Pope John Paul II has expressed the same truth with these words: "The Church wishes to serve this single end: that each person may be able to find Christ..." [751-757].

Just as Christ is the sacrament of God, the Church is your sacrament, your visible sign, of Christ. But the Church is not a sacrament "for members only." The Second Vatican Council clearly says: "Since the church, in Christ, is a sacrament—a sign and instrument, that is, of communion with God and of the unity of the entire human race—it here proposes, for the benefit of the faithful and of the entire world, to describe more clearly, and in the tradition laid down by earlier council, its own nature and universal mission" (*Dogmatic Constitution on the Church*, 1) [775, 1045].

In the plan that God has for the human race, the Church is *the* sacrament, *the* primary visible instrument, through which the Spirit is bringing about the total oneness that lies in store for us all [776].

This process of salvation, however, is a divine-human venture. We all have a part in it. Our cooperation with the Spirit consists of becoming a Church that sees Christ in others so that others see Christ in us [779].

The Catholic People of God
[781-786]

In speaking of the Church, the Second Vatican Council emphasizes the image of the people of God more than any other one [804].

Strictly speaking, all people are the people of God. In chapters 8 and 9 of Genesis, the Bible testifies that God has a covenant relationship with all of humankind [762]. But the people-of-God image applies in a special way to Christ's New Testament followers and sheds light on important features of the Catholic community [763-766].

One important fact about Catholics is this: we have a sense of *being a people*. Even though we are made up of the most varied ethnic and national groups, we have a sense of *belonging* to the same worldwide family [815].

Another thing about the Catholic people is our sense of *history*. Our family line reaches back to earliest Christianity. Few of us know the whole panorama of our history as a Church. But most of us know stories of martyrs and saints. We know of groups, ancient and modern, who have endured persecution for the faith. And deep down we identify with these people and their history. All those generations who went before us are your people and mine [813-816, 834].

Our sense of being a people goes very deep. There may be lapsed Catholics and nonpracticing Catholics. But good or bad, they are Catholics. When they want to come back, they know where home is. And when they do come home, they are welcomed. The Church has its imperfections. But at its heart is the endless stream of God's mercy and forgiveness [827].

The Catholic community is not the whole of God's people. But it is that strong, identifiable core group who realize where we are all going [834]. Like the Old Testament people trudging toward the Promised Land, we are keenly aware that "here we have no lasting city, but we seek the one that is to come" (Hebrews 13:14). Our faith instinct tells us that God is in our future and that we need one another to reach him. This is part of our strength, a facet of our mystery [2796].

The Catholic Church: A Unique Institution
[811-870]

In the Apostolic Constitution *Pastor bonus* Pope John Paul II writes, "The Good Shepherd, the Lord Christ Jesus (cf. Jn 10:11,14), conferred on the bishops, the successors of the

Apostles, and in a singular way on the bishop of Rome, the successor of Peter, the mission of making disciples in all nations and of preaching the Gospel to every creature. And so the Church was established, the people of God, and the task of its shepherds or pastors was indeed to be that service 'which is called very expressively in Sacred Scripture a *diaconia* or ministry'" (1).

From the earliest years of its history, Christianity has had a visible structure: appointed leaders, prescribed forms of worship, and approved formulas of faith. Seen in terms of these elements, the Catholic Church is a visible society. Because it is also a mystery, however, the Church is unlike any other organized group [771-779].

> *Peter is to provide the Church with unshakable leadership...*

As a visible society, the Catholic Church is unique. Other Christian churches possess some of the same basic characteristics in common with it, such as the gifts of "one Lord, one faith, one baptism; one God and Father of all" (Ephesians 4:56). But as Vatican II points out, "Since these are gifts belonging to the church of Christ, they are forces impelling towards catholic unity" (*Dogmatic Constitution on the Church,* 8) [771, 819, 827].

Furthermore—and this is a decisive point regarding the uniqueness of the Catholic Church—Vatican II states that "this church, constituted and organized as a society in the present world, *subsists in the Catholic Church...*" (*Dogmatic Constitution on the Church,* 8). This key statement teaches that the basic fullness of the Church, the vital source of complete Christian unity in the future, is found uniquely in the visible Catholic Church [816, 819, 870].

Infallibility in the Church

[889-892]

Christ gave to the Church the task of proclaiming his Good News. (See Matthew 28:19-20.) He also promised us his Spirit, who guides us "to all truth" (John 16:13). That mandate and that promise guarantee that we the Church will never fall away from Christ's teaching. This ability of the Church as a whole to avoid error regarding basic matters of Christ's teaching is called *infallibility* [2035, 2051].

The pope's responsibility is to preserve and nourish the Church. This means striving to realize Christ's Last Supper prayer to his Father, "That they may all be one, as you, Father, are in me and I in you, that they also may be in us, that the world may believe that you sent me" (John 17:21) [820]. Because the pope's responsibility is also to be a sacramental source of unity, he has a special role in regard to the Church's infallibility [936, 937].

The Church's infallibility is preserved by its key instrument of infallibility, the pope. The infallibility which the whole Church has belongs to the pope in a special way. The Spirit of truth guarantees that when the pope declares that he is teaching infallibly as Christ's representative and visible head of the Church on basic matters of faith or morals, he cannot lead the Church into error. This gift from the Spirit is called papal infallibility [891].

Speaking of the infallibility of the Church, the pope, and the bishops, Vatican II says: "This infallibility, however, with which the divine redeemer wished to endow his church in defining doctrine pertaining to faith and morals, extends just as far as the deposit of revelation, which must be religiously guarded and faithfully expounded. The Roman Pontiff, head of the college of bishops, enjoys this infallibility in virtue of his office....The infallibility promised to the church is also present in the body of bishops when, together with Peter's successor, they exercise the supreme teaching office" (*Dogmatic Constitution on the Church,* 25) [877, 935].

9. Mary, Mother of Jesus and of the Church

[484-511, 963-975]

...the Virgin Mary is the Church's model of faith and charity.

CATECHISM OF THE CATHOLIC CHURCH, 967

In his encyclical *Redemptoris Mater,* Pope John Paul II wrote, "In their midst Mary was 'devoted to prayer' as the 'mother of Jesus' (cf. Acts 1:13-14), of the Crucified and Risen Christ. And that first group of those who in faith looked 'upon Jesus as the author of salvation,' knew that Jesus was the Son of Mary, and that she was his Mother, and that as such she was from the moment of his conception and birth a unique witness to the mystery of Jesus..." (26). From that "first group" to our own day, the Church has acknowledged Mary's influence on our lives [972].

Because she is the mother of Jesus, Mary is the mother of God. As Vatican II puts it: "The Virgin Mary, who at the message of the angel received the Word of God in her heart and in her body and brought forth life to the world, is acknowledged and honored as truly the mother of God and of the Redeemer" (*Dogmatic Constitution on the Church,* 53) [484-507, 966].

As Mother of the Lord, Mary is an entirely unique person. Like her Son, she was conceived as a human being exempt from any trace of original sin. This is called her *Immaculate Conception*. Mary also remained free from personal sin during her life [490-493, 508].

Before, during, and after the birth of her son, Mary remained physically a virgin [510-511]. At the end of her life, Mary was assumed—that is, taken up—body and soul into heaven. This is called her *Assumption* [966].

As Mother of the Christ whose life we live, Mary is also the Mother of the whole Church. She is a member of the Church, but an altogether unique member. Vatican II expresses her relationship to us as "pre-eminent and as a wholly unique member of the church, and as its exemplar and outstanding model in faith and charity....The catholic church taught by the holy Spirit, honors her with filial affection and devotion as a most beloved mother" (*Dogmatic Constitution on the Church*, 53) [971].

Like a mother waiting up for her grown children to come home, Mary never stops influencing the course of our lives. Vatican II says: "She conceived, gave birth to, and nourished

Mary is the Mother of the whole Church.

Christ, she presented him to the Father in the temple, shared his sufferings as he died on the cross....For this reason she is a mother to us in the order of grace" (*Dogmatic Constitution on the Church*, 61) [484-507]. "By her motherly love she cares for her Son's sisters and brothers who still journey on earth surrounded by dangers and difficulties, until they are led into their blessed home" (*Dogmatic Constitution on the Church*, 62) [488, 968-970, 2674].

This mother, who saw her own flesh-and-blood son die for the rest of her children, is waiting and preparing your home for you. She is, in the words of Vatican II, your "sign of certain hope and comfort" (*Dogmatic Constitution on the Church,* 68).

10. The Saints

The Church also honors the other saints who are already with the Lord in heaven. These are people who have served God and their neighbors in so outstanding a way that they have been canonized. That is, the Church has officially declared that they are in heaven, holds them up as heroic models, and encourages us to pray to them, asking their intercession with God for us all [956, 957, 962].

We do not worship the saints, be we honor them as heroes. They are people like us who have achieved the goal. They are with God.

11. The Scriptures and Tradition

[80-83]

Tradition and scripture make up a single sacred deposit of the word of God, which is entrusted to the church.

DOGMATIC CONSTITUTION ON DIVINE REVELATION, 10

The Second Vatican Council describes sacred Tradition and sacred Scripture as being "like a mirror, in which the church, during its pilgrim journey here on earth, contemplates God" (*Dogmatic Constitution on Divine Revelation,* 7) [97].

God's Word of revelation comes to you through words spoken and written by human beings. "Sacred scripture is the utterance of God put down in writing under the inspiration of the holy Spirit" (*Dogmatic Constitution on Divine Revelation*, 9). Sacred Tradition is the handing on of God's Word by the successors of the apostles [95, 97].

The Bible: Its Books and Its Message
[101-141]

Sacred Scripture, the Bible, is a collection of books. According to the canon of Scripture (the Catholic Church's list of books accepted as authentic), the Bible contains 73 books. The 46 books of the Old Testament were written approximately between 900 B.C. and 160 B.C.—that is, before the coming of Christ. The 27 books of the New Testament were written approximately between A.D. 50 and A.D. 140 [120].

The Old Testament collection is made up of historical books, didactic (teaching) books, and prophetic books (containing the inspired words of prophets, people who experienced God in special ways and were his authentic spokesmen). These books, with a few exceptions, were written originally in Hebrew [121].

In brief, the Old Testament books are a record of the experience the Israelite people had of Yahweh, the God of their fathers. (Recall Exodus 3:13-15.) As a whole, these books reveal Israel's insight into the personal reality of the one God, Yahweh, who acts in human history guiding it with plan and purpose. Yahweh, the God of the Old Testament, is the same God whom Jesus, a Jew, called Father [122, 123, 128-130, 140].

The New Testament books, written originally in Greek, are made up of gospels (proclamations of the Good News) and epistles (letters). First, in the order in which they appear in the Bible, are the Gospels of Matthew, Mark, Luke, and John. The first three gospels are called *Synoptic* (from the Greek *synoptikos*, "seeing the whole together") because they tell much the same story in much the same way. The book called Acts of the Apostles, which follows the Gospel of John, is a sequel to the Gospel of Luke; written by Luke, Acts continues the narrative of his Gospel. The Gospel of John (also called the fourth gospel) fills out the view of Jesus found in the three Synoptic Gospels [125-127].

Next in sequence come the epistles of Saint Paul—the earliest New Testament documents—which were written in each case to meet particular needs of various local Christian communities.

After Paul's epistles come the Catholic epistles. These letters are called catholic, or universal, because they were not written to deal with particular needs of local churches but with matters important to all Christian communities.

The final book of the New Testament is the Book of Revelation, a message of hope for persecuted Christians, promising Christ's ultimate triumph in history [120].

The basic theme of the New Testament is Jesus Christ. Each book reveals a different side of his mystery. The four gospels record the words and deeds of Jesus as they were remembered and handed down in the early generations of the Church [139]. They tell the story of his passion and death, and what that death means in the light of his Resurrection. In a sense the gospels *began* with the Resurrection; Jesus' teachings and the events in his life made sense to the early Christians only *after* his Resurrection [638-658]. The gospels reflect the shared faith of the first Christians in the Lord who is risen and now dwells among us [124-127].

The New Testament writings tell not who Jesus *was* but who he *is*. More than mere historical documents, these writings have the power to change your life. In the New Testament "mirror" you can find Jesus Christ. If you accept what you see in that mirror, the meaning Christ has for you in your life situation, you can also find yourself [101-104, 124].

Tradition, Vatican II, and Parents
[74-83, 4-10, 1653-1658]

Sacred Tradition is the handing on of God's Word. This handing on is done officially by the successors of the apostles and unofficially by all who worship, teach, and live the faith as the Church understands it [173].

Certain ideas and customs grow out of the Tradition process and become instrumental to it, some even for a period of centuries. But a product of Tradition is a basic element in it only if that product has served to hand on the Faith in an unvarying form since the early centuries of the Church. Examples of these basic elements are the Bible (as a tangible tool used in handing on the Faith), the Apostles' Creed, and the basic forms of the Church's liturgy.

In a particular era a product of the Tradition process can play a special role in handing on the faith [74-83]. The documents of ecumenical councils are prime examples. An ecumenical council is an official meeting, for the purpose of decision making, by the bishops of the world who are in union with the pope. The teachings of an ecumenical council—

products of Tradition in the strict sense—play a decisive role in the Tradition process [884]. The documents of the sixteenth-century Council of Trent have played such a role. So have the documents of Vatican I, which took place in the nineteenth century [9].

In our time, the documents of Vatican II are playing the same role in the handing-on process. As Pope Paul VI declared in a 1966 address: "We must give thanks to God and have confidence in the future of the Church when we think of the Council: it will be *the great catechism of our times*" [10].

Vatican II has done what the teaching Church has always done: it has spelled out the unchangeable content of revelation, translating it into thought-forms of people in today's culture. But this "translation of unchangeable content" is not just old news dressed up in new language. As Vatican II has stated: "The tradition that comes from the apostles makes progress in the church, with the help of the holy Spirit. There is a *growth* in insight into the realities and words that are being passed on….As the centuries go by, the church is always advancing towards the plenitude of divine truth, until eventually the words of God are fulfilled in it" (*Dogmatic Constitution on Divine Revelation*, 8) [77-79, 98, 2650, 2651].

Through Vatican II the Church has heeded the Spirit and engaged in its "responsibility of reading the signs of the times and of interpreting them in the light of the Gospel" (*Pastoral Constitution on the Church in the Modern World,* 4). Where

> *Sacred Tradition is the handing on of God's word.*

the Spirit is leading us is not always clear. But the ground on which we the Church move forward in our pilgrimage is firm: the Gospel of Christ. At this stage in our history, one of our

45

basic instruments of Tradition—the handing on of the faith—
is the documents of Vatican II [767, 768, 810].

Tradition is an entirely personal process. The faith is
handed on *by people to people*. Popes and bishops, priests and
religious, theologians and teachers, pass on the faith. But the
main people involved in the process are parents and their
children. Children of Chinese parents seldom develop an Irish
brogue. And children of nonreligious parents seldom develop
a deep, living faith. So in regard to Tradition, keep in mind the
words of the noted English priest-educator, Canon Drinkwater:
"You educate to some extent...by what you say, more by what
you do, and still more by what you are; but most of all by the
things you love" [4-10, 902, 1653-1658, 2204-2206].

12. Sin: Original and Personal
[396-409]

*Although set by God in a state of righteousness, men
and women, enticed by the evil one, abused their freedom at the very start of history.*

PASTORAL CONSTITUTION ON
THE CHURCH IN THE MODERN WORLD, 13

The Original Sin and Its Effects

Chapters 1 and 2 of Genesis tell the story of creation by
God. God created all things, including man and woman, and
saw that they were good [279-324, 355-384].

But into this good world entered sin. In chapter 3 of
Genesis, the man, Adam, rejects God and tries to become his
equal. As a result of this original sin, the man feels alienated

from God. He hides. When God confronts him, Adam blames the woman, Eve, for his sin, and she in turn blames the serpent. The point is simple and tragic: the man's guilt has distorted all his relationships. Sin has turned life into a harsh burden [385, 397-401].

Chapters 4 through 11 of Genesis depict the escalation of sin in the world, rippling out from Adam's original sin. Cain murders his brother Abel. Sin reaches such proportions that God sends a great flood that covers the earth—a symbol of the chaos and destruction sin brought to creation. In chapter 11 human folly reaches its peak: man tries again to become God's equal by building a tower reaching to the heavens [56, 57, 60]. This rejection of God spills over into man's rejection of his fellow man. There is now division and complete lack of communication among nations [1865].

According to Genesis, a world of beauty was deformed by sin. The ongoing result has been division, pain, bloodshed, loneliness, and death. This tragic narrative has a familiar feel to it. The reality it points to is a basic part of human experience. It is no surprise that this reality—the fact of original sin and its effects—is a teaching of the Church [396-409].

With the exception of Jesus Christ and his mother Mary, every human being born into this world is affected by original sin. As Saint Paul declared in Romans 5:12, "Therefore, just as through one person sin entered the world, and through sin, death, and thus death came to all, inasmuch as all sinned" [402].

While continuing to point out that there is evil in this world, the Church does not suggest that human nature is corrupt. Rather, humankind is capable of much good. While experiencing a "downward pull," we still maintain essential control over our decisions. Free will remains [386-390]. And—most importantly—Christ our Redeemer has conquered sin and death by his death and resurrection. This victory has swallowed up not only our personal sins but the original sin and its widespread effects. The doctrine of original sin, then, is best viewed as a dark backdrop against which can be contrasted the brilliant redemption won for us by Christ our Lord [606-618].

Personal Sin

[1846-1876]

In addition to the effects of original sin, there is personal sin—sin committed by an individual. We sin personally whenever we knowingly and deliberately violate the moral law. By sinning, we fail to love God. We turn aside from—or even back away from—our lifetime goal of doing God's will [1849-1853].

A mortal sin is a fundamental rejection of God's love. By it, God's grace-presence is driven from the sinner. *Mortal* means "death-dealing." This sin kills God's life and love in the person sinning. For a sin to be mortal, there must be (1) serious matter, (2) sufficient reflection, and (3) full consent of the will [1854-1861].

Sins, of whatever seriousness, do not have to be actions.

A venial sin is a less serious rejection of God's love. *Venial* means "easily forgiven." A sin is venial if the offense is not serious or—if the matter is serious—the person is not sufficiently aware of the evil involved or does not fully consent to the sin.

Venial sin is like a spiritual sickness that hurts but does not kill God's grace-presence within the person. There can be degrees of seriousness in sinning, just as different sicknesses can be more or less serious. Even less serious sins, however, should not be taken lightly. People in love do not want to offend one another in any way, even the slightest [1862, 1863].

Sins, of whatever seriousness, do not have to be actions. A person can sin by thought or desire or by failing to do something that should be done [1849, 1871]. God will forgive any sin—even the most serious—over and over if the person is truly sorry [1864].

Those who judge themselves to be in mortal sin must be reconciled to Christ and the Church before they receive holy Communion (see 1 Corinthians 11:27-28) [1385]. A person in mortal sin can return to God's grace before confession by having perfect sorrow or contrition, but this perfect contrition must be accompanied by the intention to confess the sin and receive sacramental absolution [1452, 1455, 1456].

Personal Sin and Social Evil
[1865-1869]

Patterns of evil can be institutionalized. Injustice, for example, can become part of a group's way of life, embedded in laws and social customs. Such patterns, in a ripple effect, contaminate the attitudes and actions of people in that environment. The influence of these patterns can be so subtle that people enmeshed in them may literally be unaware of the evil they promote [1865-1869].

The mystery of original sin has a social dimension, and

cooperation in evil patterns deepens the presence of evil in the world. It contributes to human suffering. Thus, Vatican II makes a point of focusing—especially during the penitential season of Lent—on "the social consequences of sin" (*Constitution on the Sacred Liturgy,* 109).

To go along with institutional evil makes a person "part of the problem"—an active descendant of the Old Man, Adam. To resist or confront social evil makes you "part of the answer"—a person alive with the life won for us by the New Man, Jesus Christ [1869, 1872].

Formation of a Correct Conscience
[1776-1802]

The part of you that tells you right from wrong is your conscience. Within your conscience is the law God places there, and your happiness and dignity depends upon following that law. You will be judged on how well you followed your conscience: "Their conscience is people's most secret core, and their sanctuary. There they are alone with God whose voice echoes in their depths" (*Pastoral Constitution on the Church in the Modern World,* 16) [1777-1782].

We are all morally bound to follow our conscience. But this does not mean that what our conscience tells us is infallibly correct. We are required to properly form our conscience so that it will be a reliable guide. Sometimes, through no fault of our own, there are things we do not know that causes our conscience to be unreliable. As Vatican II says, "Conscience goes astray through ignorance" (*Pastoral Constitution on the Church in the Modern World,* 16). Seeking a correct conscience is part of our dignity and responsibility [1790-1794].

Speaking of a correct conscience, Vatican II states: "Hence, the more a correct conscience prevails, the more do persons and groups turn aside from blind choice and endeavor to conform to the objective standards of moral conduct" (*Pastoral Constitution on the Church in the Modern World,* 16) [1786-1789].

There are certain things you can do to properly form your conscience. The first place to look to know moral behavior is the Bible. You should also look to Church teaching which helps us understand what we read in the Bible. The Church has, over the centuries, developed principles that help us decide how to act [1785, 2032].

You can call upon the Holy Spirit to help you in your decisions, so prayer should be part of your consideration. You can ask the advice of knowledgeable people to help you know what to do [1788].

13. The Sacraments of the Church
[1210-1666]

The seven sacraments touch all the stages and all the important moments of Christian life.

CATECHISM OF THE CATHOLIC CHURCH, 1210

Baptism: New Life and Ways of Living
[1213-1284]

Through symbolic immersion in the waters of baptism, you are "grafted into the paschal mystery of Christ." In a mysterious way, you "die with him, are buried with him, and rise with him" (*Constitution on the Sacred Liturgy*, 6) [1086].

As a baptized Christian, you are an adopted brother or sister of Christ, "hid with Christ in God," but a visible member of his Body [1266].

Having died to sin (both original sin and personal sins are cleansed away in the waters of baptism) [1263, 1264], you have entered the community of the Church "as through a door." Your indelible baptism into Christ was the beginning of a unique lifelong vocation [1214-1216, 1263, 1271].

Many people exercise their baptismal calling through parish activities. Assisting their parish priests, they serve as extraordinary ministers of Communion, lectors, commentators, choir leaders, ushers, servers, members of the parish council, the Legion of Mary, the St. Vincent de Paul Society, the social justice committee, and many other parish groups [911].

Some serve the spiritual and community life of their parishes by teaching religion and taking part in adult-education programs, Scripture study, prayer groups, and family enrichment groups, such as Marriage Encounter. Many find their baptismal faith revitalized by praising God together as charismatic Catholics. These are only some of the ways in which baptized members of Christ's Body live out the mystery of their baptismal vocation [898-913].

A major way of living the life of baptism is called the religious life. Heeding a special grace from God, some people enter religious orders and congregations and become religious brothers, sisters, and priests [914-933, 944, 945].

As consecrated religious, these people dedicate themselves to God by vowing to live the evangelical counsels of poverty, chastity, and obedience. As Vatican II explains, their lives are devoted to God's service: "This constitutes a special consecration, which is deeply rooted in their baptismal consecration and is a fuller expression of it" (*Decree on the Up-to-Date Renewal of Religious Life,* 5) [930, 944, 2102, 2103].

Through your baptism, you share with others "the sacramental bond of unity among all who through it are reborn" (*Decree on Ecumenism,* 22). Your baptism can never be repeated because it binds you to God forever. The bond is unbreakable. It is possible for you to lose grace and even faith, but you cannot lose your baptism. You are marked as one of God's own. That same bond links you to all other baptized persons in a sacramental way. You are one of us and we are all "sacrament persons." Together we are called to live until death the baptismal mystery into which we have been plunged [941, 1271, 2791].

Confirmation: Seal of the Spirit, Gift of the Father
[1285-1321]

Confirmation is the sacrament by which those born anew in baptism receive the seal of the Holy Spirit, the Gift of the Father. Along with baptism and the Eucharist, confirmation is a sacrament of initiation—in this case, initiation into the life of adult Christian witness. The deepened presence of the Spirit, who comes to us in this sacrament, is meant to sustain us in a lifetime of witness to Christ and service to others [1302, 1303].

If you were being confirmed today, the celebrant would moisten his thumb with chrism, the specially blessed mixture of olive oil and balsam, and trace the sign of the cross on your forehead. This act is the laying on of hands, which is an actual part of the sacrament going back to the time of the apostles.

While anointing you, the celebrant would address you, using your new confirmation name, and say: "Be sealed with the Gift of the Holy Spirit." These words have rich connections with early Christianity. As Saint Paul wrote to the Christians in Ephesus, "In him you also…were sealed with the promised holy Spirit, which is the first installment of our inheritance…" (Ephesians 1:13-14) [1299, 1300].

The word *Gift*, used in confirmation, is spelled with a capital, because the Gift we receive in this sacrament is the Spirit himself [1293].

Eucharist: Sacrifice and Sacrament
[1322-1419]

"At the last supper, on the night when he was betrayed, our Savior instituted the eucharistic sacrifice of his body and blood. This he did in order to perpetuate the sacrifice of the cross throughout the ages until he should come again, and so to entrust to his beloved spouse, the church, a memorial of his death and resurrection: a sacrament of love, a sign of unity, a bond of charity, 'a paschal banquet in which Christ is received, the mind is filled with grace, and a pledge of future glory is given to us'" (*Constitution on the Sacred Liturgy,* 47) [1323, 1398].

This mystery is the very center and culmination of Christian life. It is the "source and the summit of all preaching of the Gospel...the center of the assembly of the faithful" (*Decree on the Ministry and Life of Priests*, 5) [1175, 1181, 1324, 1392].

> *The Eucharist draws you into the compelling love of Christ and sets you afire.*

In every Mass, Christ is present, both in the person of his priest and especially under the form of bread and wine. In every Mass, his death becomes a present reality, offered as our sacrifice to God in an unbloody and sacramental manner. As often as the sacrifice of the cross is celebrated on an altar, the work of our redemption is carried on [1333, 1350, 1372].

At Mass we offer Christ, our passover sacrifice, to God, and we offer ourselves along with him. We then receive the risen Lord, our bread of life, in holy Communion. In so doing, we enter into the very core of the paschal mystery of our salvation— the death and resurrection of Christ [1330, 1356-1359].

Eating the supper of the Lord, we span all time and "proclaim the death of the Lord until he comes" (1 Corinthians 11:26). Sharing this banquet of love, we become totally one body in him. At that moment our future with God becomes a present reality. The oneness for which we are destined is both symbolized and made real in the meal we share. In the Mass, both past and future become really present in mystery [1382-1398, 1402, 1405].

If you prepare for it with care and enter into it with living faith, the Eucharist can draw you into the compelling love of Christ and set you afire. When you go out from the sacred mystery, you know you were caught up in it if you "grasp by deed what you hold by creed." And if you return to the place where the Blessed Sacrament is kept, Christ present in the tabernacle, you can regain your sense of the fathomless love his presence there silently speaks [1066-1075, 1418].

Penance: Reconciliation
[1422-1498]

Penance is the sacrament by which we receive God's healing forgiveness for sins committed after baptism. The rite is called reconciliation because it reconciles us not only with God but with the Church community. Both these aspects of reconciliation are important [1468-1470].

As members of Christ's Body, everything we do affects the whole Body. Sin wounds and weakens the Body of Christ; the healing we receive in penance restores health and strength to the Church, as well as to ourselves.

When you confess your sins sincerely, God rejoices.

When a person turns aside or away from God's love, the harm is to the sinner. Venial sin strains one's relationship with God. Mortal sin ruptures the relationship [1854-1863].

Sin is a tragic reality. But the sacrament of penance is a joyful reunion. Chapter 15 of Luke's Gospel expresses this joy poignantly: the Pharisees accuse Jesus of being too merciful. In response, Jesus tells three parables. In the first, God is like a shepherd who leaves ninety-nine sheep to seek one who is lost. When he finds it, he is filled with joy [1443].

In the second parable, a woman finds a valuable coin she had lost and throws a big party. Jesus comments: "In just the same way, I tell you, there will be rejoicing among the angels of God over one sinner who repents" (15:10) [545-546].

The third parable is the story of the wayward son. When the son returns home, his father receives him with a tender embrace [2839].

When you confess your sins sincerely, with true sorrow and resolution not to sin again, God rejoices. The Pharisees depicted in Luke's Gospel were stern, rigid men—stricter judges than God. In contrast, the Father revealed by Jesus is almost too good to be true. And so is Jesus himself, whom you meet in this sacrament. Like Father, like Son. In penance, Jesus embraces and heals you [1441-1442].

Anointing of the Sick
[1499-1532]

In serious illness you experience mortality. You realize that at some time *you* are going to die. If you are not seriously ill, but infirm or aged, you know this same experience.

Because these circumstances lead you to face God in the light of your own death, there is something especially sacramental about the condition you are in. And so there is a formal sacrament for this sacramental situation: anointing of the sick [1522].

Anointing does not hasten the act of death. In this sacrament, however, God does invite you to commune with him in the light of your final meeting with him. Through this sacrament, the entire Church asks God to lighten your sufferings, forgive your sins, and bring you to eternal salvation [1520].

Anointing of the sick helps you to share in the cross of Christ.

57

You need not be on the verge of dying to receive this sacrament. This is clear from the fact that the anointing and the prayers that accompany it have as a purpose the restoration of health. Therefore, if you are not in immediate danger of death, but are infirm or aged, you can and should ask for the sacrament. If you ever are in danger of death, either from sickness or old age, you should not delay receiving the sacrament [1514-1515].

Anointing of the sick helps you to share more fully in the cross of Christ. By so sharing, you contribute to the spiritual good of the whole Church. By the fact that you share more fully in the cross of Christ through anointing, you are being prepared for a fuller share in Christ's Resurrection [1521].

Holy Orders:
Ministerial Priesthood
[1536-1600]

The Church is the Body of Christ. As such, the whole Church shares in the nature and tasks of Christ, our head. This includes sharing in his priesthood [787-796, 1268, 1546].

But beyond this "common priesthood of the faithful," there is the special or "ministerial" priesthood that certain members of the Church receive through the sacrament of holy orders [901, 1547].

Each type of priesthood—common or ministerial—is a sharing in the priesthood of Christ. And both types are related to each other. But there is a basic difference between them. In the eucharistic sacrifice, for example, the ordained priest acts "in the person of Christ" and offers the sacrifice to God in the name of all, and the people join with the priest in that offering. The two roles—of priest and people—go together [901-903].

Priests receive their priesthood from bishops, who possess the fullness of the sacrament of holy orders. When a bishop ordains priests, he gives them a sharing of his priesthood and mission [1562-1564].

Priests share in Christ's ministry by preaching his gospel, doing all in their power to bring their people to Christian maturity. They baptize, heal, forgive sin in the sacrament of penance, anoint the sick, and act as the Church's witness in the sacrament of matrimony. Most importantly, priests celebrate the Eucharist, which is "the center of the assembly of the faithful over which the priest presides" (*Decree on the Ministry and Life of Priests*, 5). All priests are united in the single goal of building up Christ's Body [1565-1568, 1595].

When priests are ordained, they "are signed with a special character," an interior capability that empowers them to "act in the person of Christ the head" (*Decree on the Ministry and Life of Priests,* 2). This special inner "character" unites priests in a sacramental bond with one another—a fact that, in a sense, sets them apart from other people. This "being set apart" is meant to help priests do God's work with total dedication [1581-1584].

As Vatican II points out, priests "perform other services for people" just as Jesus did (*Decree on the Ministry and Life of Priests,* 2). One thing this means is that priests need their people just as their people need them. Laypeople who work closely with priests help them to be leaders in the community of God's people [910].

In addition to bishops and priests, deacons also have a special sharing in the sacrament of holy orders. The diaconate, conferred by a bishop, is received as the first stage in ordination by those who are preparing for the priesthood. Since the Second Vatican Council, however, the ancient order of deacon has been restored in the Roman Catholic Church as an office in its own right. Many dioceses now have deacons who do not go on to become priests. They are known, therefore, as *permanent* deacons. Working under the authority of the local bishop, permanent deacons serve the people of God at the direction of priests in parishes [1569-1571, 1596].

Deacons were common in the early days of the Church and are becoming common once again in the United States. The permanent deacon is ordained to perform his ministry. Deacons may be married or unmarried members of the Church. The diaconate is a ministry of service. Their service usually combines liturgical service and pastoral service in the community.

Matrimony: Sacrament of Life-giving Oneness
[1601-1666]

In all civilizations people have sensed a mysterious sacredness about the union of man and woman. There has always been a vague realization that the deep longing for oneness with "the other" is life-giving—and that it is a longing for oneness with the source of all life. This is why religious rituals and codes of behavior have always been connected with marriage.

> *Matrimony is a sacramental vocation in and for the Church.*

Jesus made marriage the sacrament of matrimony, giving matrimony a new dimension to the Christian vocation that begins in baptism [1601].

In matrimony a husband and wife are called to love each other in a very practical way: by serving each other's most personal needs; by working seriously at communicating their personal thoughts and feelings to each other so their oneness is always alive and growing. This love is explicitly, beautifully sexual. As Vatican II points out, "Married love is uniquely expressed and perfected by the exercise of the acts proper to marriage" (*Pastoral Constitution on the Church in the Modern World,* 49) [1643-1654].

In matrimony a couple is also called to live their sacrament for others. By their obvious closeness, a couple affects the lives of others with "something special"—the love of Christ in our midst. They reveal Christ's love and make it contagious to their children and to all who come into contact with them. A major purpose, and natural outcome, of matrimony is the begetting of new life—children. But a couple's love also gives life—the life of Christ's Spirit—to other people [1652-1658, 2366, 2367].

A couple does not live a life of love because they happen to be compatible. They do it consciously and deliberately because it is their vocation and because matrimony is called "a great mystery…in reference to Christ and the church" (Ephesians 5:32) [1616].

Matrimony is much more than a private arrangement between two people. It is a sacramental vocation in and for the Church. It is a medium through which Christ reveals and deepens the mystery of his oneness with us, his Body. Thus, husbands and wives live a truly sacramental life when they follow the advice given in Ephesians 5:21: "Be subordinate to one another out of reverence for Christ" [1617].

In the Catholic Church, a couple's sacramental union is *exclusive* (one man with one woman) and *indissoluble* (till death do us part). These are concrete ways in which the mysterious oneness between husband and wife, Christ and Church, becomes reality [1643-1645, 2360-2379].

The best thing parents can do for their children is to love each other. Similarly, one of the best things a couple can do for the Church and for the world is to strive for greater closeness [2201-2231].

14. Human Destiny

[988-1060]

It is appointed that human beings die once, and after this the judgment....

HEBREWS 9:27

Individual Death and Judgment

Catholics believe in two final destinies—one for individuals and one for humankind as a whole [678-679].

Your life as an earthly pilgrim reaches its point of arrival at the moment of death. Having passed beyond the world of time and change, you can no longer choose a different reality as the ultimate love of your life. If your basic love-choice at the moment of death is the absolute Good whom we call God, God remains your eternal possession. This eternal possession of God is called heaven [1023-1029].

If your ultimate love-choice at the moment of death is

anything less than God, you experience the radical emptiness of not possessing the absolute Good. This eternal loss is called hell [1033-1037, 1056, 1057].

The judgment at the instant of death consists in a crystal-clear revelation of your unchangeable, freely chosen condition—eternal union with God, or eternal alienation [1021, 1022].

Purgatory and the Communion of Saints
[1030-1032, 954-959]

We can die in the love of God but still deserve punishment for our sins just like a person can steal something, be sorry, but still deserve punishment. This punishment we deserve might be called the "stains of sin." Such stains are cleansed away in a purifying process called purgatory. These stains of sin are primarily the temporal punishment due to venial or mortal sins already forgiven but for which sufficient penance was not done during your lifetime. This doctrine of purgatory, reflected in Scripture and developed in Tradition, was clearly expressed in the Second Council of Lyons (A.D. 1274).

Having passed through purgatory, you will be utterly unselfish, capable of perfect love. Your selfish ego—that part of you that restlessly sought self-satisfaction—will have died forever. The "new you" will be your same inner self, transformed and purified by the intensity of God's love for you.

Besides declaring the fact of purgatory, the Second Council of Lyons also affirmed that "the faithful on earth can be of great help" to persons undergoing purgatory by offering for them "the sacrifice of the Mass, prayers, almsgiving, and other religious deeds" [958, 1032, 1055].

Implied in this doctrine is the bond of oneness—called the communion of saints—that exists between the people of God on earth and those who have gone before us. Vatican II focuses on this bond of union by saying that it "accepts loyally the venerable faith of our ancestors in the living communion which exists between us and our sisters and brothers who are in the glory of heaven or who are yet being purified after their death" (*Dogmatic Constitution on the Church,* 51) [828, 959].

The communion of saints is a two-way street. In the section quoted above, Vatican II points out that just as you on earth can help those who undergo purgatory, those in heaven can help you on your pilgrimage by interceding with God [946-962].

Hell

[1033-1037]

God, who is infinite love and mercy, is also infinite justice [1040]. Because of God's justice, as well as his total respect for human freedom, hell is a real possibility as a person's eternal destiny. This side of God's mystery is difficult for us to grasp. But Christ himself taught it, and so does the Church [1861].

The teaching on hell is clearly in Scripture. Christ says to the just: "Come, you who are blessed by my Father. Inherit the kingdom prepared for you from the foundation of the world." But to the unjust he says: "Depart from me, you accursed, into the eternal fire prepared for the devil and his angels" (Matthew 25:34,41). Elsewhere, Jesus is recorded as saying: "It is better for you to enter into life maimed than with two hands to go into Gehenna" (Mark 9:43) [1056, 1057].

One point that emerges quite clearly from this doctrine is the reality of human freedom. You are free to seek God and serve him. And you are free to do the opposite. In either case you are responsible for the consequences. Life is a serious matter. The way you live it makes a serious difference. You are free, radically free, to seek God. And you are free, radically free, to choose the inexpressible pain of his absence [1730-1748].

Heaven
[1023-1029]

Grace, God's presence within you, is like a seed—a vital, growing seed that is destined one day to break forth full grown.

God has given himself to you, but in a hidden way. For the time being, you seek him even as you possess him. But the time will come when your seeking will be over. You will then see and possess God completely. This has been revealed [1024].

In his first letter, Saint John says: "Beloved, we are God's children now; what we shall be has not yet been revealed. We do know that when it is revealed we shall be like him, for we shall see him as he is" (1 John 3:2) [1720].

And in his First Letter to the Corinthians, Saint Paul says: "At present we see indistinctly, as in a mirror, but then face to face. At present I know partially; then I shall know fully, as I am fully known" (13:12) [164].

This is heaven: direct face-to-face vision of God as he is—Father, Son, and Spirit; total and perfect union with God, an ecstasy of fulfillment beyond human imagining; the "now" of eternity in which everything is ever new, fresh, and present to you; the warm flood of joy in the company of Jesus, his Mother, and all those you have ever known and loved; a total absence of pain, regret, bad memories; the perfect enjoyment of all your powers of mind and (after the resurrection on Judgment Day) of body.

This is heaven. That is to say, this is a pale, human indication of what God has promised to those who love him, of what Christ has gained for us by his death and resurrection [163, 1023, 1024, 2519].

A New Earth and a New Heaven

[1042-1050]

Belief in the Final Judgment on the last day is clearly expressed in the Creeds of the Church. On that day all the dead will be raised. Through divine power, we will all be present before God as bodily human beings [681, 682]. Then God— the absolute Lord of history—will conduct a panoramic judgment of all that humankind did and endured through the long centuries in which the Spirit struggled to bring us forth as one people [1038-1041].

When will that day come? In a remarkable passage filled with hope for all things human, Vatican II addresses this question and expresses the Church's vision: "We do not know the moment of the consummation of the earth and of humanity nor the way the universe will be transformed. The form of this world, distorted by sin, is passing away and we are taught that God is preparing a new dwelling and a new earth in which righteousness dwells, whose happiness will fill and surpass all the desires of peace arising in human hearts" (*Pastoral Con-*

stitution on the Church in the Modern World, 39) [1001, 1048, 1059, 1060].

Meanwhile, during the time that is left to us, "the body of a new human family grows, foreshadowing in some way the age which is to come" (*Pastoral Constitution on the Church in the Modern World,* 39) [1049, 2820].

After we have "spread on earth the fruits of our nature and our enterprise—human dignity, sisterly and brotherly communion, and freedom—according to the command of the Lord and in his Spirit, we will find them once again, cleansed this time from the stain of sin, illuminated and transfigured....Here on earth the kingdom is mysteriously present; when the Lord comes it will enter into its perfection" (*Pastoral Constitution on the Church in the Modern World,* 39) [1048-1050].

That kingdom is already present in mystery. The day has already begun when God "will wipe every tear from their eyes, and there shall be no more death or mourning." The day has already begun when he says to all living things: "Behold, I make all things new....They are accomplished. I [am] the Alpha and the Omega, the beginning and the end" (Revelation 21:4,5,6) [1044, 1186].

Meanwhile, we work and pray for the full flowering of that kingdom to come. With the early Christians, we cry out: *Marana tha!* Come, Lord Jesus! We seek you [1130, 1403, 2548-2550, 2853].

SECTION TWO

PRACTICES

1. God's Two
Great Commandments
[1877]

The basis of all law (your rule of life) rests on two commandments: "You shall love the Lord, your God, with all your heart, with all your soul, and with all your mind....You shall love your neighbor as yourself" (Matthew 22:37,39) [2055, 2083].

2. Commandments of God
[2084-2557]

These are an extension of the two great commandments. The first three tell you how to love your God; the rest show you how to love your neighbor [2196].

The Ten Commandments

1. I am the Lord your God; you shall not have strange gods before me [2084-2141].

2. You shall not take the name of the Lord your God in vain [2142-2167].

3. Remember to keep holy the Lord's Day [2168-2195].

4. Honor your father and your mother [2197-2257].

5. You shall not kill [2258-2330].

6. You shall not commit adultery [2331- 2400].

7. You shall not steal [2401-2463].

8. You shall not bear false witness against your neighbor [2464-2513].

9. You shall not covet your neighbor's wife [2514-2533].

10. You shall not covet your neighbor's goods [2534-2557].

3. Precepts of the Church

[2041-2043, 2048]

From time to time, the Church has listed certain specific duties of Catholics. Some of these duties are basic obligations we have as Catholics and are known as precepts of the Church.

The Precepts of the Church

- You shall assist at Mass on Sunday and Holy Days of Obligation [2042].

- You shall confess your sins at least once a year [2042].

- You shall humbly receive your Creator in Holy Communion at least during the Easter season [2042].

- You shall keep holy the Holy Days of Obligation [2043].

- You shall observe the prescribed days of fasting and abstinence [2043].

- You shall observe the marriage laws of the Church [1601-1666].

- You shall join in the missionary spirit and apostolate of the Church [2044-2046].

- You shall provide for the material needs of the Church according to your means [2043].

Observing these precepts means we have to make certain decisions. To keep holy the holy days of obligation and Sunday means that we should avoid needless work, business activities, unnecessary shopping, and so forth [1166, 1167, 1389, 2042, 2174-2192].

If we are to live a sacramental life by receiving communion and reconciliation, we must go beyond the minimum of once a year. Although our obligation is to confess our sins once a year if we have committed a serious sin, we should try to confess our sins regularly and receive holy Communion when we attend Mass whenever we are free from serious sin [1389, 1417, 2042].

Observing the marriage laws of the Church includes giving religious training to our children. Additionally, we use Catholic schools when we can and religious education programs [1656, 1657].

4. Holy Days of Obligation
[2043, 2180, 2698]

Holy days of obligation are special feasts on which Catholics who have reached the age of reason are seriously obliged, as on Sundays, to assist at Mass and to avoid unnecessary work. Serious reasons excuse us from these obligations. In the United States these days are:

Holy Days of Obligation
In the United States

1. Mary, the Mother of God, January 1

2. Ascension of our Lord

3. Assumption of Mary, August 15

4. All Saints Day, November 1

5. Immaculate Conception of Mary, December 8

6. Nativity of Our Lord, December 25

December 8 (Immaculate Conception) and December 25 (Christmas) are always holy days of obligation.

When January 1 (Mary, Mother of God), August 15 (Mary's Assumption), or November 1 (All Saints) fall on either a Saturday or Monday, Catholics in the United States are excused from the obligation to attend Mass, but the liturgical celebration always falls on the actual holy day.

The Ascension is celebrated either the fortieth day after Easter or replaces the seventh Sunday after Easter. Check with your local Catholic Church to know which day applies in your area.

5. Regulations for Fast and Abstinence

[2043]

Fast and abstinence are two common penances in the Church. There are particular times when we practice a penance together and we are obligated to fast and abstain. Other times, we can practice fast and abstinence as a personal penance. Abstinence means we do not eat meat. Ash Wednesday, Good Friday, and all the Fridays of Lent are days of abstinence. The obligation to abstain on the appointed days begins the day after your fourteenth birthday.

Fasting means that we eat only one full meal on the fast day. Ash Wednesday and Good Friday are days when we are obliged to fast. Two other light meals are permitted, but eating between meals is not permitted. You are obliged to observe the fast from the day after your eighteenth birthday until the day after your fifty-ninth birthday.

Friday is the Church's day of penance in memory of Jesus' passion. Some form of penance is especially encouraged on each Friday throughout the year [1438]. (Catholics living in Canada should consult their parish priests about Canadian regulations.)

Pregnant women and people who are sick are not obliged to fast. Others who feel they are unable to observe the laws of fast and abstinence should consult a parish priest or confessor.

Fast and abstinence are recognized forms of penance. By doing these and other penances, we can realize that interior change of heart that is so necessary for all Christians [1434-1437].

6. Confession of Sins

[1424, 1491]

The precept to confess at least once a year is a reminder to receive the sacrament of penance (reconciliation) on a regular basis. If no grave sin has been committed in that time, confession is not necessary [1493]. However, frequent confession is of great value; it makes us more deeply conformed to Christ and most submissive to the voice of the Spirit [2042].

Reconciliation is a personal encounter with Jesus Christ represented by the priest in the confessional or reconciliation room. The penitent admits to God that he or she has sinned, makes an act of sorrow, accepts a penance (prayers, acts of self-denial, or works of service to others), and resolves to do better in the future [983, 986, 1441, 1442].

There are different ways to celebrate the sacrament of reconciliation. One common way is outlined here, but it may be different in your parish. Remember, the priest will always help you.

After prayer and an examination of conscience to find out what sins you have committed, you enter the confessional [1450-1460].

- Father greets you kindly.
- You respond and then make and say the Sign of the Cross.
- Father invites you to have confidence in God.
- You answer, "Amen."
- Father may read or recite some short selection from the Bible.

- You introduce yourself (not by name) and tell how long it has been since your last confession. You then tell your sins. (Each mortal sin must be confessed as well as possible.) It is useful to mention your most frequent and most troublesome venial sins.
- Father will give you any necessary advice and answer your questions. After he assigns a penance *you* make an Act of Contrition (see page 89).
- Father then places his hands on your head (or extends his right hand toward you) and prays these words of forgiveness:

God, the Father of mercies, through the death and resurrection of his Son has reconciled the world to himself and sent the Holy Spirit among us for the forgiveness of sins; through the ministry of the Church may God give you pardon and peace, and I absolve you from your sins in the name of the Father, and of the Son, and of the Holy Spirit.

- You answer, "Amen."
- Father then says, "Give thanks to the Lord, for he is good."
- You answer, "His mercy endures for ever."
- Father then dismisses you in these or similar words, "The Lord has freed you from your sins. Go in peace."

(For further information on penance, see page 56.)

7. Regulations for the Communion Fast

[1387, 1415]

The conditions for receiving holy Communion are the state of grace (freedom from mortal sin), the right intention (not out of routine or human respect but for the purpose of pleasing God), and observance of the Communion fast.

This fast means that you must not eat anything or drink any liquid (other than water) one hour before the reception of Communion. However, the sick and aged, even those not confined to bed or a home (and those caring for them who wish to receive Communion but cannot fast for an hour without inconvenience), can receive holy Communion *even if they have taken something during the previous hour.*

8. How to Receive Communion

[1384-1390, 1415-1417]

During Mass, you have the opportunity to receive Communion if you are in the state of grace. Each Bishop can establish rules in his own diocese, but most follow a common practice. The ceremony outlined below is from the General Instruction of the Roman Missal (#160). Remember, things may be slightly different in your parish or diocese.

You will usually receive Communion standing. Holy Communion may be received on the tongue or in the hand and may be given under the form of bread alone or under both species [1390].

When you receive Communion, you bow your head

before the Sacrament as a gesture of reverence. If you receive under the species of bread and wine, then you make the same gesture of reverence when receiving the Body of Christ and again when you receive the Blood of Christ.

When the minister addresses the communicant with the words "The Body of Christ," "The Blood of Christ," the communicant responds "Amen" to each.

When the minister raises the eucharistic bread or wine, this is an invitation for the communicant to make an Act of Faith, to express his or her belief in the Eucharist, to manifest a need and desire for the Lord, to accept the good news of Jesus' paschal mystery.

A clear, meaningful, and purposeful "Amen" is your response to this invitation. In this way, you openly profess your belief in the presence of Christ in the eucharistic bread and wine, as well as in his Body, the Church.

9. Beatitudes
[1716-1717]

A mature, adult Christianity involves more than obedience to laws. Those who follow Christ and live by his Spirit know that their salvation rests on struggle and pain. The beatitudes are a summary of the difficulties to be overcome by faithful Christians and the rewards that will be theirs if they are loyal followers of Christ (Matthew 5:3-10).

The Beatitudes
[1716]

- Blessed are the poor in spirit, for theirs is the kingdom of heaven.

- Blessed are they who mourn, for they shall be comforted.

- Blessed are the meek, for they shall inherit the earth.

- Blessed are they who hunger and thirst for righteousness, for they shall be satisfied.

- Blessed are the merciful, for they shall obtain mercy.

- Blessed are the pure in heart, for they shall see God.

- Blessed are the peacemakers, for they shall be called sons of God.

- Blessed are they who are persecuted for righteousness' sake, for theirs is the kingdom of heaven.

- Blessed are you when men revile you and persecute you and utter all kinds of evil against you falsely on my account.

Rejoice and be glad, for your reward is great in heaven (see Matthew 5:3-12).

Here is a shorter version of the beatitudes:

1. Happy are those who need God.
2. Happy are those with self-control.
3. Happy are those who are sorry for sin.
4. Happy are those who hunger and thirst for holiness.
5. Happy are the merciful.
6. Happy are those who love with all their heart.
7. Happy are the peacemakers.
8. Happy are those who suffer for doing what is right.

10. Corporal (Material) Works of Mercy
[2443, 2447]

1. To feed the hungry.
2. To give drink to the thirsty.
3. To clothe the naked.
4. To visit the imprisoned.
5. To shelter the homeless.
6. To visit the sick.
7. To bury the dead [1681-1690, 2300].

11. Spiritual Works of Mercy
[2443, 2447]

1. To admonish the sinner.
2. To instruct the ignorant.
3. To counsel the doubtful.
4. To comfort the sorrowful.
5. To bear wrongs patiently.
6. To forgive all injuries.
7. To pray for the living and the dead [958, 1032].

12. How to Baptize in Case of an Emergency

[1240-1256, 1284]

Pour ordinary water on the forehead (not the hair) of the person to be baptized, and say while pouring it: "I baptize you in the name of the Father, and of the Son, and of the Holy Spirit."

(Note: Any person can and should baptize in case of necessity; the same person must say the words while pouring the water.)

13. How to Prepare for a Sick Call
(Reconciliation, Communion, Anointing)

[1517-1519]

Be sure to call the parish or a priest whenever a relative or friend has become seriously ill. The person does not have to be in danger of death. It is quite common for the sick person to receive holy Communion, which may be received at any hour. The bishop, priest, deacon, or communion minister may bring Communion to the sick. If the bishop or priest visits, the person may also receive the sacraments of reconciliation and anointing of the sick.

Cover a small table with a cloth. If possible, have the table near the bed or chair of the sick person. A crucifix and a vessel of holy water should be provided as well as candles.

Communion to the sick may be received at any hour. If the sick person cannot receive the Eucharist under the form of bread, it may be given under the form of wine alone. Those who care for the sick may also receive Communion.

When the bishop, priest, deacon, or communion minister arrives, lead him or her to the sick person. If the bishop or priest is the one who visits and the sick person wishes to receive the sacrament of penance you should leave the room to give them privacy. After reconciliation is finished, return and join in the prayers.

14. Liturgical Seasons of the Year

[1163-1173]

Through the liturgy, the work of our redemption is exercised. It is "through the liturgy, especially, that the faithful are enabled to express in their lives and manifest to others the mystery of Christ and the real nature of the true Church" (*Constitution on the Sacred Liturgy*, 2). It is "the summit toward which the activity of the Church is directed; it is also the fount from which all her power flows" (*Constitution on the Sacred Liturgy*, 10) [2698].

On appointed days in the course of the year, the Church celebrates the memory of our redemption by Christ. Throughout the year, the entire mystery of Christ is unfolded. The Church does this in sequence during the various seasons of the liturgical year [1166].

Advent: This season begins four weeks (or slightly less) before Christmas [524]. (The Sunday which falls on or closest to November 30 is its starting point.)

Christmas Season: This season lasts from Christmas until the Baptism of the Lord, the Sunday after Epiphany. (The period from the end of Christmas Season until the beginning of Lent belongs to *Ordinary Time*.) [1171]

Lent: The penitential season of Lent lasts forty days, beginning on Ash Wednesday and ending before the Mass of the Lord's Supper on Holy Thursday. The final week is called Holy Week. The Paschal Triduum begins with the Mass of the Lord's Supper and ends after evening prayer on Easter Sunday [540, 1438].

Easter Season: This season, whose theme is resurrection from sin to the life of grace, lasts fifty days, from Easter to Pentecost [1096, 1168, 1169].

Ordinary Time: This season comprises the thirty-three or thirty-four weeks in the course of the year that celebrate no particular aspect of the mystery of Christ. Instead, the mystery of Christ in all its fullness is celebrated. It includes not only the period between the end of the Christmas Season and the beginning of Lent but also all the Sundays after Pentecost to the last Sunday of the liturgical year (Christ the King) [1166, 1167, 2177].

PRAYERS

[2559-2565, 2697-2699]

Introductory Note

According to an ancient definition, prayer is "keeping company with God." Prayer is *you* relating to God in the deepest recesses of your personality. It is you seeking and communing with the living God—responding to him as he has made himself known to you through the teachings of the Church.

As intimately personal as it is, prayer makes use of word formulas. Liturgical prayer—the official community prayer of the Church—uses approved formulas. So does unofficial group prayer. Even in solitary private prayer, traditional formulas can be of great help.

At its most personal, private prayer is spontaneous or impromptu—and sometimes even wordless. Nonetheless, formulas are practical helps for breaking into prayer and expressing faith. For this reason some of the most loved, time-approved formulas of Catholic devotion are offered here—prayers that express the whole range of prayerful attitudes:

adoration, thanksgiving, petition, and atonement. Also offered in this section is a suggested method of private meditative prayer [2700-2704].

There are prayers that Catholics learn from their youngest days. The following are those basic Catholic prayers.

1. Sign of the Cross
[232-237]

In the name of the Father, and of the Son, and of the Holy Spirit. Amen. *(Said at the beginning and end of prayers.)*

2. Our Father
[2759-2865]

Our Father, who art in heaven, hallowed be thy name; thy kingdom come; thy will be done on earth as it is in heaven. Give us this day our daily bread; and forgive us our trespasses as we forgive those who trespass against us; and lead us not into temptation, but deliver us from evil. Amen.

3. Hail Mary
[2676, 2677]

Hail Mary, full of grace. The Lord is with thee. Blessed art thou among women, and blessed is the fruit of thy womb, Jesus. Holy Mary, Mother of God, pray for us sinners, now and at the hour of our death. Amen.

4. Prayer of Praise (Doxology)

[2639-2643]

Glory to the Father, and to the Son, and to the Holy Spirit; as it was in the beginning, is now, and will be for ever. Amen.

5. Grace Before and Thanksgiving After Meals

[2698]

Bless us, O Lord, and these your gifts, which we are about to receive from your bounty, through Christ, our Lord. Amen.

We give thanks for all your benefits, almighty God, who lives and reigns forever. May the souls of the faithful departed, through the mercy of God, rest in peace. Amen. (Spontaneous prayers may also be used at mealtime.)

Catholics treasure many prayers and use them throughout their lives. Her are some common Catholic prayers.

6. Morning Offering

[2659-2660]

Most holy and adorable Trinity, one God in three Persons, I praise you and give you thanks for all the favors you have bestowed on me. Your goodness has preserved me until now. I offer you my whole being and in particular all my thoughts, words, and deeds, together with all the trials I may undergo this day. Give them your blessing. May your divine love animate them and may they serve your greater glory.

I make this morning offering in union with the divine intentions of Jesus Christ who offers himself daily in the holy sacrifice of the Mass, and in union with Mary, his Virgin Mother and our Mother, who was always the faithful handmaid of the Lord. Amen.

or

Almighty God, I thank you for your past blessings. Today I offer myself—whatever I do, say, or think—to your loving care. Continue to bless me, Lord. I make this morning offering in union with the divine intentions of Jesus Christ who offers himself daily in the holy sacrifice of the Mass, and in union with Mary, his Virgin Mother and our Mother, who was always the faithful handmaid of the Lord. Amen.

7. Act of Faith
[1814-1816, 2656]

O my God, I firmly believe that you are one God in three divine Persons, Father, Son, and Holy Spirit; I believe that your divine Son became man and died for our sins, and that he will come to judge the living and the dead. I believe these and all the truths which the holy Catholic Church teaches, because you revealed them, who can neither deceive nor be deceived. Amen.

8. Act of Hope
[1817-1821, 2657]

O my God, relying on your infinite goodness and promises, I hope to obtain pardon of my sins, the help of your grace, and life everlasting, through the merits of Jesus Christ, my Lord and Redeemer. Amen.

9. Act of Love
[1822-1829, 2658]

O my God, I love you above all things, with my whole heart and soul, because you are all good and worthy of all my love. I love my neighbor as myself for the love of you. I forgive all who have injured me and I ask pardon of all whom I have injured. Amen.

10. Act of Contrition
[1450-1460]

(a) My God, I am sorry for my sins with all my heart. In choosing to do wrong and failing to do good, I have sinned against you whom I should love above all things. I firmly intend, with your help, to do penance, to sin no more, and to avoid whatever leads me to sin. Our Savior Jesus Christ suffered and died for us. In his name, my God, have mercy. Amen.

(b) O my God, I am sorry for my sins because I have offended you. I know I should love you above all things. Help me to do penance, to do better, and to avoid anything that might lead me to sin. Amen.

(c) Any spontaneous and heartfelt prayer that tells God that you are truly sorry for all your sins, that you will mend your ways, and that you firmly intend to avoid what leads to sin is a good Act of Contrition.

11. Come, Holy Spirit

[2670-2672]

Come, Holy Spirit.
**Response: Fill the hearts of your faithful and make the
fire of your love burn within them.**

Send forth your spirit and there shall be another creation.
Response: And you shall renew the face of the earth.

Let us pray: O God, you have instructed the hearts of the
faithful by the light of the Holy Spirit. Grant that through the
same Holy Spirit we may always be truly wise and rejoice in
his consolation. Through Christ our Lord. Amen.

12. Prayer for Vocations

[914-933, 2004]

O Jesus, send laborers into your fields, which are awaiting
holy apostles, saintly priests, heroic missionaries and dedi-
cated sisters and brothers. Enkindle in the hearts of men and
women the spark of a vocation. Grant that Christian families
may desire to give to your church, helpers in the work of
tomorrow. Amen. (Pope John XIII)

13. Prayer to Your Guardian Angel

[335, 336, 350-352]

Angel of God, my guardian dear, to whom his love commits
me here, ever this day (night) be at my side, to light and guard,
to rule and guide. Amen.

14. Prayer for the Faithful Departed

[958, 1032]

Eternal rest grant unto them, O Lord.
Response: And let perpetual light shine upon them.

May their souls and the souls of all the faithful departed, through the mercy of God, rest in peace.
Response: Amen.

15. Stations of the Cross

[617, 1674]

Meditations on the Suffering and Death of Jesus

Introductory Prayer

Jesus, I wish to take this walk to Calvary with you. I know that you suffered for love of me. Help me always to love you.

At each station, contemplate the scene and pray a brief, heartfelt prayer.

1. Jesus is condemned to death on the cross.
2. Jesus accepts his cross.
3. Jesus falls the first time.
4. Jesus meets his sorrowful Mother.
5. Simon of Cyrene helps Jesus carry his cross.
6. Veronica wipes the face of Jesus.
7. Jesus falls the second time.
8. Jesus meets and speaks to the women of Jerusalem.
9. Jesus falls the third time.
10. Jesus is stripped of his garments.

11. Jesus is nailed to the cross.

12. Jesus dies on the cross.

13. Jesus is taken down from the cross.

14. Jesus is placed in the tomb.

Closing Prayer (recalling the Resurrection)

16. Prayer to
Jesus Christ Crucified

[618]

Behold, my beloved and good Jesus. I cast myself upon my
knees in your sight, and with the most fervent desire of my soul
I pray and beseech you to impress upon my heart lively
sentiments of faith, hope, and charity, with true repentance for
my sins and a most firm desire of amendment; while with deep
affection and grief of soul I consider within myself and
mentally contemplate your five most precious wounds, having before my eyes that which David the prophet long ago
spoke about you, my Jesus: "They have pierced my hands and
my feet; / I can count all my bones" (Psalm 22:17-18).

17. Prayer to Our Redeemer

[1381]

Soul of Christ, sanctify me; body of Christ, save me.
Blood of Christ, inebriate me;
Water from the side of Christ, wash me.
Passion of Christ, strengthen me. O good Jesus, hear me.
Within your wounds hide me. Never permit me to be separated
from you. From the evil one protect me, at the hour of death

call me, and bid me come to you that with your saints I may praise you forever. Amen.

Devotion to Mary the Mother of God is a basic part of Catholic spirituality. The following are some common Marian prayers.

18. Memorare
[2673-2675, 2679]

Remember, O most gracious Virgin Mary, that never was it known that anyone who fled to your protection, implored your help, or sought your intercession was left unaided. Inspired with this confidence, I fly to you, O virgin of virgins, my Mother. To you I come, before you I stand, sinful and sorrowful. O Mother of the Word Incarnate, despise not my petitions, but in your mercy, hear and answer me. Amen.

19. Angelus
[973, 2617]

The angel of the Lord declared unto Mary.
Response: And she conceived of the Holy Spirit.
(Hail Mary)

Behold the handmaid of the Lord.
Response: May it be done unto me according to your word.
(Hail Mary)

And the Word was made flesh.
Response: And dwelt among us.
(Hail Mary)

Pray for us, O holy Mother of God.
Response: That we may be made worthy of the promises of Christ.

Let us pray: O Lord, it was through the message of an angel that we learned of the Incarnation of Christ, your Son. Pour your grace into our hearts, and by his Passion and cross bring us to the glory of his Resurrection. Through Christ, our Lord. Amen.

20. Queen of Heaven

[972-975, 2617-2622]

(Prayer during the Easter Season instead of Angelus)

Queen of Heaven, rejoice, alleluia.
Response: The Son whom you were privileged to bear, alleluia, has risen as he said, alleluia. Pray to God for us, alleluia.

Rejoice and be glad, Virgin Mary, alleluia.
Response: For the Lord has truly risen, alleluia.

Let us pray: O God, it was by the Resurrection of your Son, our Lord Jesus Christ, that you brought joy to the world. Grant that through the intercession of the Virgin Mary, his Mother, we may attain the joy of eternal life. Through Christ, our Lord. Amen.

21. Hail, Holy Queen

[963-975, 2617-2622, 2672-2675]

Hail, holy queen, mother of mercy, our life, our sweetness, and our hope. To you we cry, poor banished children of Eve; to you we send up our sighs, mourning and weeping in this valley of tears. Turn then, O most gracious advocate, your eyes of mercy toward us, and after this our exile, show unto us the blessed fruit of your womb, Jesus. O clement, O loving, O sweet virgin Mary.

Pray for us, O holy Mother of God.
Response: That we may be made worthy of the promises of Christ.

Let us pray: O God, whose only begotten Son, by his life, death, and resurrection, has purchased for us the rewards of eternal life, grant, we beseech you, that meditating upon these mysteries of the most holy rosary of the Blessed Virgin Mary, we may imitate what they contain and obtain what they promise. Through the same Christ our Lord. Amen.

22. Mary's Rosary

[971, 1674, 2678, 2708]

The complete rosary is composed of twenty decades, divided into four distinct parts, each containing five decades. The first part consists of five joyful events in the life of Jesus and Mary, the second part recalls events from Jesus' ministry that illuminate his mission, the third considers sorrowful events, and the fourth part considers five glorious events.

We begin by making the Sign of the Cross.

Then we say the Apostles' Creed, one Our Father, three Hail Marys, and one Glory to the Father (Prayer of Praise) on the small chain. Then recall the first mystery, say one Our Father, ten Hail Marys, and one Glory to the Father. This completes one decade. All the other decades are said in the same manner with a different mystery meditated during each decade. At the end of the rosary, the prayer Hail, Holy Queen may be recited.

The mysteries of the rosary are scenes from the life of Jesus and Mary. By meditating on these sublime truths, we come to a better understanding of our religion: the Incarnation and ministry of the Lord, the Redemption, and the Christian life—present and future.

The Joyful Mysteries

1. The messenger of God announces to Mary that she is to be the Mother of God.

2. Mary visits and helps her cousin Elizabeth.

3. Mary gives birth to Jesus in a stable in Bethlehem.

4. Jesus is presented in the Temple.

5. Jesus is found in the Temple

The Luminous Mysteries

1. Jesus is baptized in the Jordan.

2. Jesus' self-manifestation at the wedding in Cana.

3. Jesus proclaims the kingdom of God.

4. Jesus' Transfiguration.

5. Jesus institutes the Eucharist as the sacramental expression of the paschal mystery.

The Sorrowful Mysteries

1. Jesus undergoes his agony in the Garden of Gethsemane.

2. Jesus is scourged at the pillar.

3. Jesus is crowned with thorns.

4. Jesus carries the cross to Calvary.

5. Jesus dies on the cross for our sins.

The Glorious Mysteries

1. Jesus rises from the dead.

2. Jesus ascends into heaven.

3. The Holy Spirit comes to the apostles and the Blessed Mother.

4. The Mother of Jesus is taken into heaven.

5. Mary is crowned queen of heaven and earth.

Here are two common expressions of our Catholic faith.

23. The Nicene Creed
[198-1065]

We believe in one God, the Father, the Almighty, maker of heaven and earth, of all that is seen and unseen. We believe in one Lord, Jesus Christ, the only Son of God, eternally begotten of the Father, God from God, Light from Light, true God from true God, begotten, not made, one in Being with the Father. Through him all things were made. For us men and for our salvation he came down from heaven: by the power of the Holy Spirit, he was born of the Virgin Mary, and became man. For our sake he was crucified under Pontius Pilate; he suffered, died, and was buried. On the third day he rose again in fulfillment of the Scriptures; he ascended into heaven and is seated at the right hand of the Father. He will come again in glory to judge the living and the dead, and his kingdom will have no end. We believe in the Holy Spirit, the Lord, the giver of life, who proceeds from the Father and the Son. With the Father and the Son he is worshiped and glorified. He has spoken through the Prophets. We believe in one holy catholic and apostolic Church. We acknowledge one baptism for the forgiveness of sins. We look for the resurrection of the dead, and the life of the world to come. Amen.

24. Apostles' Creed
[198-1065]

I believe in God, the Father almighty, creator of heaven and earth. I believe in Jesus Christ, his only Son, our Lord. He was conceived by the power of the Holy Spirit and born of the Virgin Mary. He suffered under Pontius Pilate, was crucified, died, and was buried. He descended to the dead. On the third day he rose again. He ascended into heaven, and is seated at the right hand of the Father. He will come again to judge the living and the dead. I believe in the Holy Spirit, the holy catholic Church, the communion of saints, the forgiveness of sins, the resurrection of the body, and the life everlasting. Amen.

The Eucharist is at the heart of Catholic faith and worship. In addition to Mass, we have other eucharistic devotions.

25. Benediction of the Most Blessed Sacrament
(Prayer to Christ in the Eucharist)
[1381]

As Catholics, it is our privilege to participate in offering the eucharistic sacrifice and in receiving holy Communion. But there are many additional acts of devotion that help extend Christ's real presence among us. Such a devotion is Benediction of the Most Blessed Sacrament.

Christ's promise is to be with us *always* (Matthew 28:20). The practice of reservation of the Blessed Sacrament arose early in the history of the Church. (This was for the convenience of the sick—that Communion might be taken to them.)

People then began spontaneously to gather in the churches to pray and worship in the very presence of Christ. Later, because Christ's presence meant so much to them, they asked that the host be exhibited to them on a throne in a monstrance (an ornamental receptacle). Still later, prayers and songs were added, and the priest would bless the people with the host enthroned in the monstrance.

Benediction is an amazingly simple and beautifully proportioned act of worship. We begin by *contemplating* God's presence in our midst. (Most of the time we are so busy talking or doing things or going places that Christ hardly gets a chance to say anything to us. Contemplation means that we let God "soak into us.") Then follows the actual sacramental blessing: the priest makes the Sign of the Cross over us with the host enshrined in the monstrance. Finally, we make our spontaneous response in words of praise and thanksgiving.

While the congregation sings an opening song (any eucharistic hymn), the celebrant removes the host from the tabernacle, places it in a monstrance, and enthrones it on the altar. After he incenses the host (a symbolic action indicating our prayerful worship), a period of silent contemplation or public prayer ensues. Then, after the homily (if there is one), a hymn such as "Down in Adoration Falling" is sung.

The celebrant then says or sings a prayer such as the following:

Celebrant: Lord Jesus Christ, you gave us the Eucharist as the memorial of your suffering and death. May our worship of this sacrament of your body and blood help us to experience the salvation you won for us and the peace of the kingdom where you live with the Father and the Holy Spirit, one God, for ever and ever.

People: Amen.

The celebrant blesses the people with the host and then returns the Eucharist to the tabernacle. Afterward the people themselves may say or sing an acclamation such as the Divine Praises [2639-2643]:

Blessed be God.
Blessed be his holy name.
Blessed be Jesus Christ, true God and true man.
Blessed be the name of Jesus.
Blessed be his most Sacred Heart.
Blessed be his most Precious Blood.
Blessed be Jesus in the most Holy Sacrament of the Altar.
Blessed be the Holy Spirit, the Paraclete.
Blessed be the great Mother of God, Mary most holy.
Blessed be her holy and Immaculate Conception.
Blessed be her glorious Assumption.
Blessed be the name of Mary, Virgin and Mother.
Blessed be Saint Joseph, her most chaste spouse.
Blessed be God in his angels and in his saints.

26. Order of the Mass
(Community Prayer)

[1345-1355]

Introductory Rites
Entrance Song
Greeting
Penitential Rite
Gloria
Opening Prayer

Liturgy of the Word
(We hear and respond to the Word of God.)
First Reading
Responsorial Psalm
Second Reading
Alleluia or Gospel Acclamation
Gospel
Homily
Profession of Faith (Creed)
General Intercessions (Prayer of the Faithful)

Liturgy of the Eucharist
(We offer Jesus to the Father.)
Preparation and Offering of Gifts
Prayer Over the Gifts
Eucharistic Prayer (Our gifts of bread and wine become
the body and blood of Christ.)
Memorial Acclamation
Lord's Prayer
Sign of Peace

Breaking of the Bread
Reception of Communion
Prayer After Communion

Concluding Rites
Blessing
Dismissal

The prayers we say in community must be supported by our private prayer.

27. A Method of Meditation
(Private Prayer)
[2705-2708, 2723]

I. Preparation

As a remote preparation try to remain conscious of God as you go about your daily schedule. Frequently remind yourself of this truth: God is everywhere and is very interested in your welfare.

At the beginning of the meditation, make a deliberate Act of Faith regarding God's presence. Ask him for pardon of any faults. Ask for help to make a good meditation. Add a prayer to our Blessed Mother and other favorite saints for assistance.

II. Consideration

Read for a few minutes from the Bible or other spiritual book. Ask yourself *What have I read? What does it teach me?*

How have I acted in regard to this till now? What shall I do about it in the future?

Since the advantage of meditation is not so much in the thinking as in the praying that it leads to, it is important to devote the greater part of meditation to affections (short prayers from the heart), petitions (requests for help from God), and resolutions (practical plans for changing your life, with God's help).

Affections: "Lord, I am sorry for having offended you." "Thank you for the blessings you have given me." "I want to love you above all things." "I praise you, Lord!" "Your will be done!" "I place my trust in you."

Petitions: Ask for whatever you need: for example, forgiveness of sins, greater confidence, help in a stressful situation, specific graces to forgive someone, to be more patient, to die a good death.

Resolutions: Make them short and specific, for example, to stop gossiping with…, to be kind to…, not to lose patience with…, to be faithful to times of prayer.

III. Conclusion

1. Thank God for the insights and graces gained during this meditation.
2. Repeat your resolutions.
3. Ask for help to keep your resolutions.
4. Choose some special thought or short prayer to carry with you during the day.

Further Suggestions
for Meditative Prayer

[2709-2719, 2724]

1. Do not do all the talking yourself. Stop now and then to listen to the Lord. The inspirations he gives on occasion are wordless insights or sentiments that you "hear" in your heart.

2. Do not try to *feel* the acts of love and other affections you express. They are acts of your will and usually do not spill over into felt emotions. If you experience dissatisfaction because your mind keeps wandering, have patience with yourself. Enduring this inability to pray is a valuable part of your prayer.

3. If you are drawn at times to thinking about or looking silently at God—or you become vaguely aware of his presence—simply go along that way. But if you find your mind wandering, return to expressing affections such as love, praise, sorrow. Some people maintain this simple focus on God by slowly repeating a phrase—for example, "Lord Jesus Christ, have mercy on me"—or a single word such as "God" or "Jesus."

SECTION FOUR

LIVING THE FAITH IN THE SPIRIT OF VATICAN II

Ecumenical councils in the Church are important affairs. They influence the Church for generations to come. We in the Church today, feel the influence of the bishops gathered in councils around the pope from the time of the Council of Jerusalem through Vatican Council II, the most recent council in the history of the Church. Each council has imparted a lasting influence in the Church, even after the name of the council is remembered only by historians.

The era that immediately follows a council is often one of turmoil. We can look back, for example, to Vatican Council I and think the doctrine of infallibility was of little controversy in the Church. In fact, there was a schism following that council and many difficult years about the interpretation of a doctrine that we accept today.

The Second Vatican Council has also produced turmoil and discussion within the Church. Since it is our most recent council, it does provide us with some basic understanding of the Church and the things that are important in the life of the Church. In that council, the Church asked us to remember yesterday, but live today. With that in mind, it is good to remember the major influences of the council that we see in the Church today.

Sacred Scripture

[101-141]

Scripture in the Life of the Church and the Believer

[131-133]

Sacred Scripture along with Tradition, form the single deposit of revelation from God. One goal the council had was to encourage all Catholics to study the Scriptures, learn from them, and use them for personal prayer. The Church gives us guidance, but we must learn and question and choose the Word of God to be alive within us.

Catholics have always been encouraged to know and study the Scriptures. Today that knowledge comes from formally or informally studying Scripture as well as being nourished by Scripture in the homily at Mass. We should prepare to hear the Scripture at Mass by reading, praying, and studying beforehand. Many parishes have adult courses on Scripture as part of their ongoing religious education.

In a sense, we can say that the Scriptures have been rediscovered by the laity after Vatican Council II. They were never really lost, but now methods exist which were not present before that can make the science of the Scripture available to young and old alike. Knowledge of the Scriptures can only strengthen our faith.

The Church teaches us that God reveals through Scripture and uses human authors to do it. We "…must take into account the conditions of their time and culture, the literary genres in use at that time, and the modes of feeling, speaking and narrating then current" [110]. If we are to do this, then we must study.

This is only one principle of interpretation, however. We must also remember that Scripture is the inspired Word of God. We need to call upon the Spirit to help us understand. This is not just personal inspiration, but the living Tradition of the Church. Interpretation of Scripture can never contradict the truths that are revealed.

Catholics should embrace the Scriptures. We do not need to fear the "science" of Scripture, for that is the very science relied upon by the Magisterium. If we read, study, and pray the Scriptures, then we will always be ready to hear the prompting that the Spirit makes in our lives.

The Interpretation of Scripture and Fundamentalism

[115-119]

There are few things that divide Christians more than the interpretation of sacred Scripture. Those who hold for the literal interpretation of Scripture are called fundamentalists. Sometimes Catholics can be at a disadvantage, if they do not know the Scriptures, when they encounter fundamentalists.

Catholics themselves can be "fundamentalist" in some of their interpretations of Scripture. Everything in Scripture is inspired, but not everything is *literal*. Robert Frost used to say that he couldn't wait for the critics to read his poems so that he could find out what he really meant. We want to know the meaning of Scripture and, like poetry, the meaning is not contained wholly in the words.

Fundamentalism is a common part of our society. We should avoid fundamentalism in our interpretation of Scripture. We should also avoid it in interpretation of dogma. The Church has clearly stated the meaning of dogma and the way we should interpret Scripture. We should turn to that source when we are in doubt.

The Bible Is a Prayer Book
[131-133]

For many years, the Bible was the only prayer book of the Church. It is the Scripture that the Fathers of the Church used for their meditation. The early religious took the Bible into the desert with them as they followed the path to perfection.

The accessibility of Scripture depended upon the literacy of the people. In the modern age, in most parts of the world, there is a high degree of literacy. The Council encouraged all people in the Church to turn to Scripture for knowledge of Christ and in search of holiness.

We can make the Bible our prayer book, too. Like many clerics and religious, we can turn to the psalms for our prayers of praise, worship, and petition. We can also use the Bible for mental prayer, which we should all try to practice. We have many collections of beautiful prayers that have been written over the years. That should not discourage us from turning to the Bible for inspiration as we pray to God. To read and think about what we read is an opportunity for God to communicate with us.

Liturgy and Worship

[1136-1209, 1322-1419]

One of the visible effects of the Second Vatican Council is the renewal of liturgy and worship within the Church. Liturgy, the way we worship, frequently evolves in the Church. The worship of the Mass involves an essential core, Scripture and Eucharist, and ritual that surrounds this core. Sometimes the ritual has been quite simple and other times, complex.

Liturgy is closely connected to the culture in which the worship occurs. Vatican Council II encouraged experimentation within the liturgy. The Council fathers wanted the Catholic faithful to clearly understand and participate in the worship of the Church. The liturgy of the Church in the United States today looks much different from the liturgy prior to Vatican Council II.

Celebration of Mass

[1345-1355]

Our celebration of Mass still includes Scripture and Eucharist. There is an opportunity, now, for laypeople to be ministers at Mass. The priest, the leader of prayer, looks for assistance from the members of the community to read the Scriptures, lead the music, assist with distributing holy Communion where appropriate, and a number of things that lead to greater participation by the worshiping community.

The celebration of Mass in the United States today is a

beautiful and prayerful experience, even though it is different from the beauty and prayerfulness of our celebration prior to Vatican Council II. There has been a new translation of the Scriptures approved for use during Mass. This translation has been included in a Lectionary, or book of readings, that all use. There are clear norms for celebrating Mass set fourth in the *General Instruction of the Roman Missal.*

There are four parts to a dignified Eucharistic celebration. The celebration begins with the Introductory Rites. Here is included all of the things that occur before the readings of the Mass. In this part we have an entrance rite where the priest and ministers enter the sanctuary to the entrance chant. The celebrant reverences the altar and greets the people. We have a penitential rite, recalling God's mercy and asking forgiveness for our sins. The invocation, "Lord, have mercy" is used during this penitential rite or immediately after it. On appropriate days we sing the prayer, Glory to God, and then join all these prayers into the opening prayer for Mass.

During this part of the Mass, the community joins in the chants and songs. The faithful prepare themselves for what they are to do in recalling their sins and asking for mercy. The worshiping community not only listens to the opening prayer, but joins their prayer to it.

The second part is the Liturgy of the Word. Here the Word of God is proclaimed. We listen to the Word and allow it to take root within us. We join in the response between the readings and with active anticipation, stand to hear the Gospel proclaimed. We listen to the homily, drawn from the Scripture of the day, and apply it to our lives. As a community we stand to profess our faith and pray fervently for the needs of the Church, the world, our country, and ourselves.

The Liturgy of the Eucharist follows the Liturgy of the Word and is the third part of the Mass. Jesus becomes present under the forms of bread and wine and we have the opportunity to receive our Lord in holy Communion. We join in the songs as the gifts are brought to the altar and prepared for the sacrifice. In the Eucharistic Prayer we listen and respond at appropriate times, for it is during this prayer that the great miracle occurs—the bread and wine become the body and blood of Christ. We join together in the prayer Jesus gave us and offer one another the peace of Christ. We approach the altar to receive holy Communion, usually standing, and with a reverent bow we receive our Lord.

The fourth part is the Concluding Rite. We sing our songs and sit silently to contemplate the great Communion we have with our God. We pray with the priest in thanksgiving for what we have received and, after the dismissal, we go out to live a life of faithful service to God and to the people of God.

The Sacraments

[1113-1134, 1210-1666]

The Holy Mass is not the only liturgy in the Church. At Vatican Council II, the bishops also called for a renewal of our celebration of the sacraments. The members of the council wanted all the faithful to be able to participate, with under-standing, in the celebration of the sacraments. We can group the seven sacraments together in three main divisions: The Sacraments of Initiation, the Sacraments of Healing, and the Sacraments of Vocation.

The Sacraments of Initiation are baptism, confirmation, and Eucharist. These are the sacraments that adult catechumens, who have never been baptized, receive upon entering the Church. They initiate us into the Christian life. For those in the Church from their infancy, the initiation is gradual, taking place usually over many years. In the United States we follow the custom of infant baptism shortly after birth and at about the age of seven, first reconciliation followed by first Eucharist. Finally, confirmation completes the initiation when the child is older.

The Sacraments of Healing are the anointing of the sick and reconciliation. Reconciliation now offers the Catholic an opportunity for a personal, face to face meeting with the priest, or the anonymity that was commonly practiced prior to Vatican Council II. The anointing of the sick is now a sacrament that Catholics can receive when they need grace and strength due to illness or advanced age. Before the work of Vatican Council II, this anointing was commonly received only by those near death. Now, anyone with a serious illness or advanced age is encouraged to receive this sacrament.

The Sacraments of Vocation are marriage and holy orders. Religious life is one of the vocations in the Church and the sacrament of religious life as well as the single life is baptism. Marriage and holy orders are sacraments meant to emphasize these two important vocations within the Church—married life and the ministerial priesthood.

The sacraments have a key role in the life of Catholics. We should receive holy Communion and reconciliation often. Also, we should not be afraid to receive the sacrament of anointing when we need it. The sacraments often provide special grace to do what we should do. For example, marriage and holy orders have special graces to help one live as a married person or as a deacon, priest, or bishop.

There are some sacraments that can only be received once. Baptism, confirmation, and holy orders have a unique effect that can occur only once. It is unusual to receive marriage more than once, although it is possible, for example after the death of a spouse. The anointing of the sick is received when you have that particular need for healing and grace.

The two sacraments Catholics receive the most are holy Communion and reconciliation. It is good to have a regular practice of reconciliation. In this sacrament, we must examine our lives and in that examination we learn our sins, but also we learn the areas of our life where we especially need God's help. We might celebrate reconciliation weekly, monthly, or several times throughout the year. Celebrating it frequently helps us keep track of our need for God in our lives. The requirement of the Church is that we receive reconciliation once a year if we have committed a mortal sin. Receiving this sacrament more frequently, however, can do nothing but help us.

We should try to receive holy Communion whenever we attend Mass. There are even times when we may receive holy Communion more than once on the same day. A person might, for example, go to daily Mass and later that day to a celebration of confirmation. In each case, the person may receive Communion. This sacrament joins us to Jesus himself. There is no other sacrament that unites us with Jesus in quite the same way. Frequent reception of holy Communion helps us live a good life and love God and others.

Called to Ministry

Jesus Christ came to save us. That was his mission. Jesus shares his mission with us when we are baptized. The way we live our lives and the service we perform in the Church, are part of the mission Jesus shares with us. The United States Catholic Bishops remind us that we have four calls. They name them as holiness, mission, community, and ministry.

Ministry is not an option for us. Service to others or to the Church, which is what ministry means, is a part of what we are called to do as Catholics. We do not all have the same ministry, however. Vatican Council II opened many ministries or avenues of service to laypeople once again. The Church emphasizes the "importance of the laity's witness and service within the family and within the professional, social, political, and cultural life of society" (*Called and Gifted for the Third Millennium*).

There are some who are full-time ministers in the Church. Many of these full-time ministers are associated with parish liturgy. Those who work for the Church, such as secretaries, directors of religious education, those working for the diocese, and catechists—to name a few—perform a service to the people of God by doing their jobs. Performing the corporal or spiritual works of mercy are a ministry to others, too.

Some special ways of serving are open to all people in the Church. The music ministry, the extraordinary minister of Communion, the reader at Mass, and the designated ministries of lector and acolyte are available to laypeople. The lector reads the word of God at Mass and also teaches it. The acolyte prepares the altar for the sacrifice of the Mass and assists the priest at the altar. Part of the contribution we make to our parish is to serve in these ministries when we are able.

Not only is ministry something we offer to God, but it is also a way of becoming holy. We must weave Catholicism into our daily lives. Participating in these ministries helps to sanctify us. Baptism is our call to ministry. We will spend our whole lives answering that call. As the United States bishops write, "Finally, we urge Catholic laity to bring Christ's peace and justice to the world by working energetically to reclaim national concern for the common good" (*Called and Gifted for the Third Millennium*).

Social Justice
[1928-1948]

"Catholics are called by God to protect human life, to promote human dignity, to defend the poor and to seek the common good. This social mission of the Church belongs to all of us. It is an essential part of what it is to be a believer." The Catholic bishops in the United States wrote these words in 1999 in their reflection, *Everyday Christianity: To Hunger and Thirst for Justice.*

Jesus is always on the side of the poor and powerless. He preaches among the poor and offers them hope. He calls upon us to respond to the needs of the poor.

Our world seems increasingly divided between the affluent and the poor. The Church at Vatican Council II responded to this division by calling upon all Catholics to be people of justice. We cannot stand by while our brothers and sisters are exploited, while their needs are ignored, and while they are killed by genocide.

This is a problem for the whole world to address. Catholics, though, have an obligation to bring attention to injustice, whether it is personal or corporate injustice. We must not only speak about justice, but we must also act. When we make investments in companies, we should look for those companies that do not take advantage of workers. They should be companies that contribute to the ethic of life. We cannot be part of corporate greed.

We Catholics must work to eliminate hunger, disease, and the causes of destitute poverty in our country and our world. That means we are accountable to God about how we use our resources, and to call others to fulfill their obligation to justice. Catholics may not be racist nor may they hate others because they are different. This is not only our personal position, but we challenge the institutions of society to examine how they contribute to injustice in the world and then to change their behavior.

Catholics are called upon to influence the values of society. Society speaks of being practical and living in the real world. The real world is God's world. It is the creation of the Father. We must be an example of that among the people with whom we live and in all the things we do.

Adult Faith Formation
[13, 162, 2088, 2087]

We must be learners our entire lives. To know the things we need to know and to live the lives we are supposed to live, we must constantly prepare. We cannot end our study of the faith when we leave childhood behind. The religious education of children and teenagers only provides a starting point. We must continue our formation throughout our adult years.

As adult Catholics we want a mature, adult faith. This kind of faith has responsibilities attached to it. These responsibilities do not end at the church door, but reach into every facet of our lives. Without a mature and nurtured faith we cannot meet our responsibilities in the Church today.

We are people of faith *and* reason. One is not at war with the other. Our knowledge helps us understand our faith. The more we know about God and church doctrine, the stronger our faith can grow. If we keep ourselves from knowing, then our faith is small and immature. We want a healthy, vibrant faith, and that means we must continue to form our faith into our adult years. If we are to fulfill our responsibilities as Catholics and understand what the Church says to us in Vatican Council II, we have to seriously consider how we will nourish our faith.

The Catholic bishops of the United States have created a pastoral plan for adult faith formation. It gives encouragement for faith formation, guidelines, and a plan for how to accomplish this formation. The spirit of Vatican Council II is evident throughout the plan. The bishops note that "Adults need to question, probe, and critically reflect on the meaning of God's revelation in their unique lives in order to grow closer to God. A searching faith leads to deepening conversion" (*Our Hearts Were Burning Within Us,* 52). The plan lists three major goals of faith formation that parishes and individual should strive towards.

The first goal is a conversion to Jesus and holiness of life. Adults should be invited to this conversion and to the search for holiness. Through homilies, parish preaching events, adult education classes, and other means, the invitation is given and suggestions for growth in holiness are made. Members of the Catholic community are called to aid each other in the growth toward holiness.

The second goal is active membership in the Christian community. Adult faith formation is not only knowledge, it is also action. Existing parish organizations and new ones where appropriate will provide the avenue for active membership. Catholics are called to look beyond minimum requirements for calling oneself Catholic, and look for ways to participate in the life of the Christian community.

The third goal is being a disciple of Jesus, participating in his mission to the world. As Catholics, we have a mission to share Jesus with the world. The continuing formation of adults makes this call clear and helps prepare them for the mission. We are called as ministers of evangelization and justice. Our ongoing formation makes it possible to take our place as a disciple of Jesus.

One method parishes use to promote both adult faith formation and evangelization is small church communities. Small groups of Catholics come together to share their faith, and under trained leadership, to continue their formation as adult Catholics. Pope John Paul II calls such communities a great hope for the Church, when such basic communities live in unity with the Church.

Pope John Paul II notes that the Synod of Bishops calls upon leaders in the local Church to foster small communities "where the faithful can communicate the Word of God and express it in service and love to one another; these communities are true expressions of ecclesial communion and centers of evangelization, in communion with their pastors" (*Christifideles Laici,* 26).

We must take the tasks of seeking and growing in faith seriously. Faith is the living gift of God and we are responsible for nourishing this living gift. The bishops highlight five of the ways this nourishment can take place. They list them as: being familiar with revelation—both Scripture and Tradition—through frequent reading, and also reading the documents of the Church; involvement in the life and mission of the Church; prayer; working for justice and serving the poor; and an active practice of loving God and neighbor.

This is indeed a life-long plan. When we incorporate this plan into our lives, we involve ourselves in an important discussion about faith and God's place in our lives. We live our faith actively as we seek to have it grow and develop within us.

Evangelization

[904-914]

As we develop and live our faith, we understand our need and obligation to bring the good news of Jesus Christ into the world where we live. We support the work of spreading the gospel with our resources and with our active involvement. Pope John Paul II has written that in this time, after Vatican Council II, we, the people of God, are aware of a renewed outpouring of the Spirit of Pentecost. We, the Church, are sent into the world to spread the Good News (see *Christifideles Laici,* 2).

In that same Apostolic Exhortation, it is clear that the call to go into the vineyard to work (see Matthew 13:38) is addressed to all members of the Church. We cannot look upon the work of spreading the Good News as the work only of the clergy and religious in the Church. We can participate in the task to spread the Good News in many ways. We do not need to look far across the oceans for the opportunity to spread the Good News. We can find the opportunity right where we live.

Spread the Good News
[4-10, 821, 905]

Evangelization, at its core, is our example of faithfully living the Christian life. Our lives are a proclamation of the presence of Christ in the world. When we act according to our belief, then we engage in the work of evangelization. Evangelization is meant to announce the Good News of Jesus to those who have never heard it, to renew the message of Jesus among the baptized, and to work for unity among believers.

There is no more effective way of doing all three than to faithfully live the life Jesus shares with us. Hypocrisy is something we must always avoid. To avoid it, we must live by the principles that Jesus taught, even when the values of our society are different. Our lifestyle, then, becomes a clear proclamation of the Word and power of God. It is also an encouragement to all believers.

For our lives to be an effective witness, we must engage in our daily life. We continue our active involvement in society that has professional, political, and cultural dimensions. We are not only interested in Church services, but in service to the people among whom we live and work. We must live in society as faithful Christians, not separated from society. As the United Sates Catholic Bishops put it, we must "connect worship on Sunday to work on Monday" (see *Everyday Christianity: To Hunger and Thirst for Justice*).

To Announce the Good News— the RCIA

[1232, 1233, 1247-1249, 1285]

One way in which we see two elements of evangelization come together is in the Rite of Christian Initiation of Adults (RCIA). In this process, not only is the Good News announced to those who have not heard it, but it also renews the message of Jesus among the baptized. The RCIA is the common way for new adult members of the Christian community to join the Church.

In some cases, this process of initiation instructs those who are not Christian, leading them to the sacrament of baptism. In other cases, Christians from other churches wish to become members of the Catholic Church. For them, the instruction is a renewal of the message of Jesus that leads to a profession of faith as a Catholic.

There are many ways to become involved in this evangelization process. One person might seek out those who show interest or curiosity about Catholicism. These people may not have a community of believers, but know they need one. An invitation may be the very thing for which they are waiting. Another person might be part of the instruction team that is part of this process. Still others might volunteer to share the story of their faith in God or be sponsors for the participants of the RCIA.

The Rite of Christian Initiation of Adults is a gradual process that takes place over many months, or in some cases, years. The first part of this process involves catechists (instructors), members of the Catholic community, and inquirers getting to know each another. This is a stage of asking questions, seeking answers, and sharing stories of faith.

Some inquirers may go no further than the first stage. For those who continue on, however, they become catechumens (people learning about the Church). For this stage catechumens are given a sponsor who will be with them during the whole process of instruction. The sponsor provides a personal witness of faith to the catechumen. Sponsors also participate with the catechumens in the liturgical life of the Church.

Those who move to the third stage make a public commitment to come into the Church. In public ceremonies, they declare their intention to be among the elect—those chosen for membership in the Church. During the season of Lent, they are introduced to the community, given the profession of faith, and examined about their beliefs and intentions. This stage ends at the Easter Vigil on Holy Saturday when the elect become members of the Church either through baptism or by making a profession of faith. Those who are baptized are also confirmed and receive the Eucharist. All three sacraments of initiation are given at this time.

The final stage of the RCIA calls upon the new Catholics to become involved in the ministry of the parish. They continue their instruction in the faith as they become fully incorporated into the community.

Unity Among Believers

[816, 830]

The third basic element of evangelization is to work for unity among believers. We can only create unity when there is mutual respect and understanding. The Second Vatican Council wrote about and encouraged ecumenism.

In the world today, people make many different responses

in faith. Over the years, Christianity has become divided over many issues. Some of these divisions run deep and have lasted for centuries. We cannot heal the fractured body of Christ, however, if we fight with each other. Catholics are called to reach out in understanding to other faiths, even though the teachings of these faiths are different from their own.

We honor the fact that people believe in God, particularly other Christians. We make sure that our beliefs are deeply rooted and try to understand what others believe. The Church calls upon all of us to treat others with respect, no matter what they believe. We may not agree with them, but they are also the children of God and have the same dignity that we do.

If we establish a neighborly relationship with other believers, we can have a conversation about our different beliefs. We do not wish to push people away, but invite them to the Church, primarily by the example of our lives. The leaders of the Church, beginning with the pope, are working hard for the unity of Christians. As faithful Catholics, in the spirit of Vatican Council II, we must do our part.

In the Spirit of the Council

"The principal task entrusted to the Council by Pope John XXIII was to guard and present better the precious deposit of Christian doctrine in order to make it more accessible to the Christian faithful and to all people of good will. For this reason the Council was not first of all to condemn the errors of the time, but above all to strive calmly to show the strength and beauty of the doctrine of the faith. 'Illumined by the light of this Council', the Pope said, 'the Church...will become greater in spiritual riches and, gaining the strength of new energies therefrom, she will look to the future without fear...Our duty is...to dedicate ourselves with an earnest will and without fear to that work which our era demands of us, thus pursuing the path which the Church has followed for 20 centuries'" (*Fidei Depositum, John Paul II*).

The Second Vatican Council provided a direction for the Church in the modern age. This direction calls upon all, lay and cleric alike, to take their place in the great task of the Church. To live in the spirit of Vatican Council II, is to live faithfully our Catholic lives. The fidelity involves educating ourselves so that we can choose—intentionally—the faith Jesus taught us as passed on to us by his body, the Church. We are the people of God. We are called to live in that dignity. Our faith comes to us from Jesus himself. In every era and culture the message of Jesus is relevant. In our own day we must allow our faith to shine through in all we do and in all we are.

Also from Liguori Publications...

Handbook for Today's Catholic Teen

This companion volume addresses issues relevant to 21st century teenagers. The breezy, friendly tone discusses serious issues in a teem appropriate manner. The major sections confirm Catholic doctrine, practices, prayers, and the theology behind them. The book ends with a direct and lively discussion of Catholic Christian moral issues that doesn't avoid the hard topics like violence, media, sex, substance abuse, and issues of conscience. An invitation for Catholic teens to take the next step into maturity. **ID# 39075 • $4.95**

Handbook for Today's Catholic Children
(formerly *You and God: Friends Forever*)

Patterned after *Handbook for Today's Catholic*, this booklet will entertain, inform, and inspire children in the ways of the faith. In a world that offers little to help children identify their roots and traditions, the booklet will foster Catholic identity and lasting faith. **ID# 39080 • $3.95**

Also available in Spanish
Guía Católica para los creyentes más pequeños
ID# 72310 • $3.95